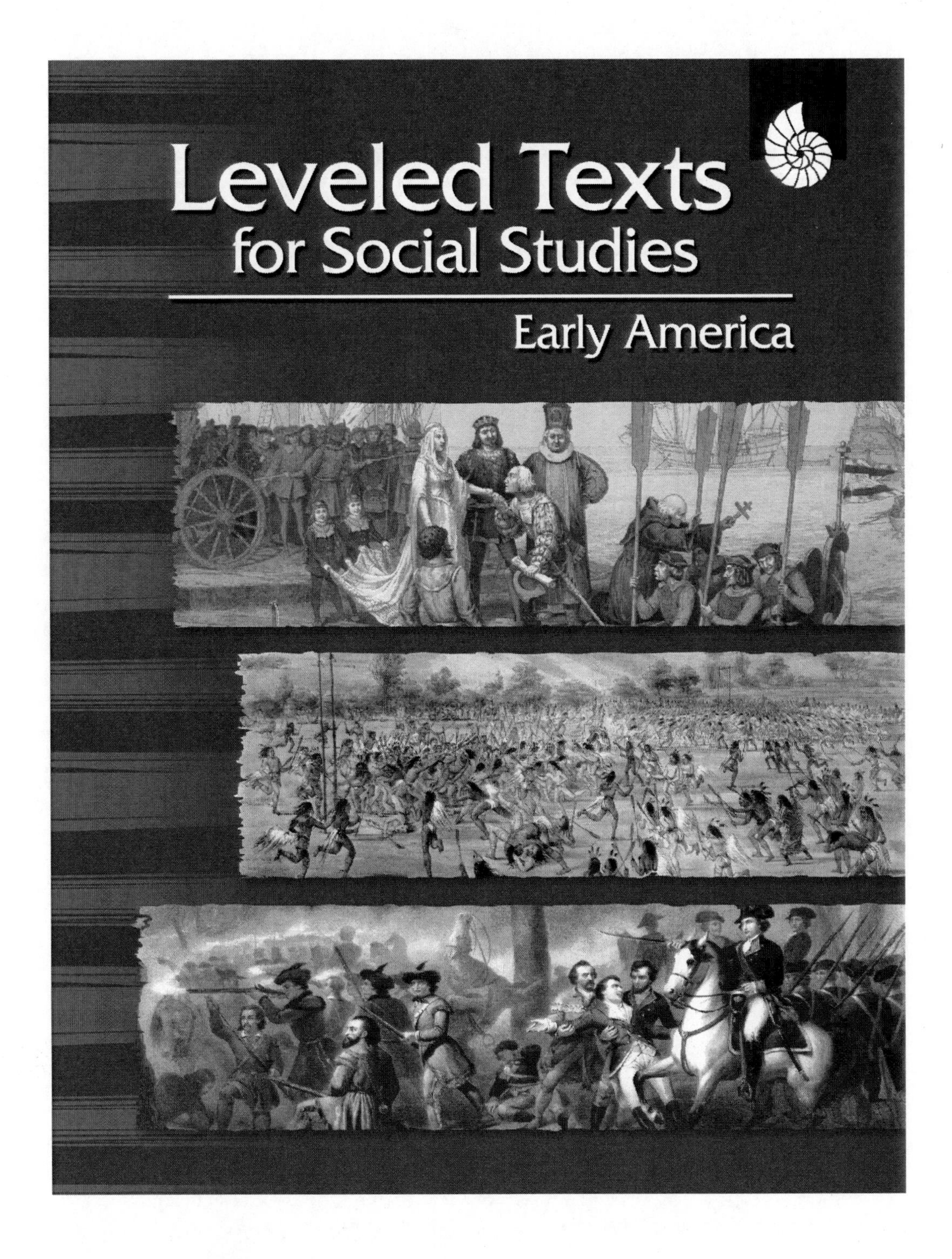
Leveled Texts
for Social Studies
Early America

SHELL EDUCATION

Reading Level Consultant
Debra J. Housel, M.S.Ed.

English Language Learner Consultant
Marcela von Vacano
Arlington County Schools, Virginia

Gifted Education Consultant
Wendy Conklin, M.A.
Mentis Online
Round Rock, Texas

Special Education Consultant
Dennis Benjamin
Prince William County
Public Schools, Virginia

Contributing Content Authors
Roben Alarcon, M.A.Ed.
Wendy Conklin, M.A.
Jill K. Mulhall, M.Ed.
Christi E. Parker, M.A.Ed.
Marie Patterson, M.S.Ed.
Emily R. Smith, M.A.Ed.

Publisher
Corinne Burton, M.A.Ed.

Associate Editor
Christina Hill, M.A.

Editorial Assistant
Kathryn R. Kiley

Editorial Director
Emily R. Smith, M.A.Ed.

Editor-in-Chief
Sharon Coan, M.S.Ed.

Editorial Manager
Gisela Lee, M.A.

Creative Director
Lee Aucoin

Cover Designer
Neri Garcia

Cover Art
Library of Congress

Imaging
Don Tran
Sandra Riley
Lesley Palmer

Shell Education

5301 Oceanus Drive
Huntington Beach, CA 92649

http://www.shelleducation.com

ISBN 978-1-4258-0081-9

Reprinted 2011

Table of Contents

Introduction

Leveled Texts

Appendix

What Is Differentiation?

Over the past few years, classrooms have evolved into diverse pools of learners. Gifted students, English language learners, special needs students, high achievers, underachievers, and average students all come together to learn from one teacher. The teacher is expected to meet their diverse needs in one classroom. It brings back memories of the one-room schoolhouse during early American history. Not too long ago, lessons were designed to be one size fits all. It was thought that students in the same grade level learned in similar ways. Today, we know that viewpoint to be faulty. Students have differing learning styles, come from different cultures, experience a variety of emotions, and have varied interests. For each subject, they also differ in academic readiness. At times, the challenges teachers face can be overwhelming, as they struggle to figure out how to create learning environments that address the differences they find in their students.

What is differentiation? Carol Ann Tomlinson at the University of Virginia says, "Differentiation is simply a teacher attending to the learning needs of a particular student or small group of students, rather than teaching a class as though all individuals in it were basically alike" (2000). Differentiation can be carried out by any teacher who keeps the learners at the forefront of his or her instruction. The effective teacher asks, "What am I going to do to shape instruction to meet the needs of all my learners?" One method or methodology will not reach all students.

Differentiation encompasses what is taught, how it is taught, and the products students create to show what they have learned. When differentiating curriculum, teachers become the organizers of learning opportunities within the classroom environment. These categories are often referred to as content, process, and product.

- **Content:** Differentiating the content means to put more depth into the curriculum through organizing the curriculum concepts and structure of knowledge.
- **Process:** Differentiating the process requires the use of varied instructional techniques and materials to enhance the learning of students.
- **Product:** When products are differentiated, cognitive development and the students' abilities to express themselves improves.

Teachers should differentiate content, process, and product according to students' characteristics. These characteristics include students' readiness, learning styles, and interests.

- **Readiness:** If a learning experience aligns closely with students' previous skills and understanding of a topic, they will learn better.
- **Learning styles:** Teachers should create assignments that allow students to complete work according to their personal preferences and styles.
- **Interests:** If a topic sparks excitement in the learners, then students will become involved in learning and better remember what is taught.

How to Differentiate Using This Product

The leveled texts in this series help teachers differentiate social studies content for their students. Each book has 15 topics, and each topic has a text written at four different reading levels. (See page 19 for more information.) These texts are written at a variety of reading levels, but all the levels remain strong in presenting the social studies content and vocabulary. Teachers can focus on the same content standard or objective for the whole class, but individual students can access the content at their *instructional* levels rather than at their *frustration* levels.

Determining your students' instructional reading levels is the first step in the process. It is important to assess their reading abilities often so they do not get tracked into one level. Below are suggested ways to use this resource, as well as other resources in your building, to determine students' reading levels.

- **Running records:** While your class is doing independent work, pull your below-grade-level students aside, one at a time. Individually have them read aloud the lowest level of a text (the star level) as you record any errors they make on your own copy of the text. If students read accurately and fluently and comprehend the material, move them up to the next level and repeat the process. Following the reading, ask comprehension questions to assess their understanding of the material. Assess their accuracy and fluency, mark the words they say incorrectly, and listen for fluent reading. Use your judgment to determine whether students seem frustrated as they read. As a general guideline, students reading below 90% accuracy are likely to feel frustrated as they read. There are also a variety of published reading assessment tools that can be used to assess students' reading levels with the running record format.
- **Refer to other resources:** Another way to determine instructional reading levels is to check your students' Individualized Education Plans, ask the school's resource teachers, or review test scores. All of these resources should be able to give you the further information you need to determine at which reading level to begin your students.

Teachers can also use the texts in this series to scaffold the content for their students. At the beginning of the year, students at the lowest reading levels may need focused teacher guidance. As the year progresses, teachers can begin giving students multiple levels of the same text to allow them to work independently to improve their comprehension. This means each student would have a copy of the text at his or her independent reading level and instructional reading level. As students read the instructional-level texts, they can use the lower texts to better understand the difficult vocabulary. By scaffolding the content in this way, teachers can support students as they move up through the reading levels. This will encourage students to work with texts that are closer to the grade level at which they will be tested.

General Information About the Student Populations

Below-Grade-Level Students

By Dennis Benjamin

Gone are the days of a separate special education curriculum. Federal government regulations require that special needs students have access to the general education curriculum. For the vast majority of special needs students today, their Individualized Education Plans (IEPs) contain current and targeted performance levels but few short-term content objectives. In other words, the special needs students are required to learn the same content objectives as their on-grade-level peers.

Be well aware of the accommodations and modifications written in students' IEPs. Use them in your teaching and assessment so they become routine. If you hold high expectations of success for all of your students, their efforts and performances will rise as well. Remember the root word of *disability* is *ability.* Go to the root of the special needs learner and apply good teaching. The results will astound and please both of you.

English Language Learners

By Marcela von Vacano

Many school districts have chosen the inclusion model to integrate English language learners into mainstream classrooms. This model has its benefits as well as its drawbacks. One benefit is that English language learners may be able to learn from their peers by hearing and using English more frequently. One drawback is that these second-language learners cannot understand academic language and concepts without special instruction. They need sheltered instruction to take the first steps toward mastering English. In an inclusion classroom, the teacher may not have the time or necessary training to provide specialized instruction for these learners.

Acquiring a second language is a lengthy process that integrates listening, speaking, reading, and writing. Students who are newcomers to the English language are not able to process information until they have mastered a certain number of structures and vocabulary words. Students may learn social language in one or two years. However, academic language takes up to eight years for most students.

Teaching academic language requires good planning and effective implementation. Pacing, or the rate at which information is presented, is another important component in this process. English language learners need to hear the same word in context several times, and they need to practice structures to internalize the words. Reviewing and summarizing what was taught are absolutely necessary for English language learners.

General Information About the Student Populations *(cont.)*

English Language Learners *(cont.)*

Oral language proficiency is the first step in the language learning process. Oral language is defined as speaking and listening skills. English language learners are able to attain word level skills (decoding, word recognition, and spelling) regardless of their oral language proficiency. However, an English language learner's ability to comprehend text and to develop writing skills is dependent on his or her oral language proficiency. Therefore, "vocabulary knowledge, listening comprehension, syntactic skills and the ability to handle meta-linguistic aspects of language, such as being able to provide the definitions of words, are linked to English reading and writing proficiency" (August and Shanahan 2006). First language oral proficiency has a positive impact on developmental patterns in second language speech discrimination and production, intra-word segmentation, and vocabulary.

On-Grade-Level Students

By Wendy Conklin

Often, on-grade-level students get overlooked when planning curriculum. More emphasis is usually placed on those who struggle and, at times, on those who excel. Teachers spend time teaching basic skills and even go below grade level to ensure that all students are up to speed. While this is a noble thing and is necessary at times, in the midst of it all, the on-grade-level students can get lost in the shuffle. We must not forget that differentiated strategies are good for the on-grade-level students, too. Providing activities that are too challenging can frustrate these students, and on the other hand, assignments that are too easy can be boring and a waste of their time. The key to reaching this population successfully is to find just the right level of activities and questions while keeping a keen eye on their diverse learning styles.

There are many ways to differentiate for this population. Strategies can include designing activities based on the Multiple Intelligence theory. Current brain research points to the success of active learning strategies. These strategies provoke strong positive emotions and use movement during the learning process to help these students learn more effectively. On-grade-level students also benefit from direct teaching of higher-level thinking skills. Keep the activities open-ended so that these students can surprise you with all they know. The strategies described on pages 9–17 were specifically chosen because they are very effective for meeting the needs of on-grade-level students as well as special populations.

General Information About the Student Populations *(cont.)*

Above-Grade-Level Students

By Wendy Conklin

In recent years, many state and school district budgets have cut funding that has in the past provided resources for their gifted and talented programs. The push and focus of schools nationwide is proficiency. It is important that students have the basic skills to read fluently, solve math problems, and grasp science concepts. As a result, funding has been redistributed in hopes of improving test scores on state and national standardized tests. In many cases, the attention has focused only on improving low test scores to the detriment of the gifted students who need to be challenged.

Differentiating through the products you require from your students is a very effective and fairly easy way to meet the needs of gifted students. Actually, this simple change to your assignments will benefit all levels of students in your classroom. While some students are strong verbally, others express themselves better through nonlinguistic representation. After reading the texts in this book, students can express their comprehension through different means, such as drawings, plays, songs, skits, or videos. It is important to identify and address different learning styles. By assigning more open-ended assignments, you allow for more creativity and diversity in your classroom. These differentiated products can easily be aligned with content standards. To assess these standards, use differentiated rubrics.

All students should be learning, growing, and expanding their knowledge in school. This includes gifted students, too. But they will not grow and learn unless someone challenges them with appropriate curriculum. Doing this can be overwhelming at times, even for the experienced teacher. However, there are some strategies that teachers can use to challenge the gifted population. These strategies include open-ended questions, student-directed learning, and using tiered assignments. (See pages 16–17 for more information about each of these strategies.)

Strategies for Using the Leveled Texts

Below-Grade-Level Students

By Dennis Benjamin

KWL Chart

Too often, below-grade-level students fall prey to low expectations. In some classrooms, below-grade-level students even buy into this negative mentality. They begin to reply "I don't know" when they are asked any question. The **KWL** strategy empowers students to take back ownership over their learning. This strategy can be used as a prereading strategy with the texts in this book. **K** stands for What I ***Know***. This first part of the process allows students to access prior knowledge and begin to make connections to the new learning about to take place. For example, when asked what they **K**now about explorers, students will reply with responses such as Columbus, ships, gold, and oceans.

The astute teacher praises the special needs students for how much they know about explorers and challenges them with the What Do You ***Want*** to Know? column. Encourage the students to create meaningful questions that cannot be answered with simply yes or no. Initially the teacher may model the questions, but ultimately students need to generate their own questions such as: Why did they explore? and How big were the explorers' ships? Now, the students have set a purpose for reading nonfiction. The reading is no longer about what the teacher wants or expects. Inquisitive minds have been opened to discover what the texts have to offer.

The **L** is for What I ***Learned***. After reading, the students should get back into a group to complete this third column. Students should then record the answers to the questions they wrote and any important concepts they learned from the text. Some students may benefit from identifying the source of information by writing such terms as text, classroom talk, or homework after each entry. That way, they can remember from where their answers came. Take the time to correct any misconceptions.

Once completed, it is important for the teacher to validate students' responses as they review the KWL chart. Praise the students for all the effort they put into the chart and highlight that they, as the learners, were responsible for its completeness and accuracy. This final step is important to help empower your below-grade-level students and encourage them to care more about their own learning.

Strategies for Using the Leveled Texts *(cont.)*

Below-Grade-Level Students *(cont.)*

Vocabulary Scavenger Hunt

Another prereading strategy is a Vocabulary Scavenger Hunt. Students preview the text and highlight unknown words. Students then write the words on specially divided pages. The pages are divided into quarters with the following headings: *Definition*, *Sentence*, *Examples*, and *Nonexamples*. A section called *Picture* is put over the middle of the chart.

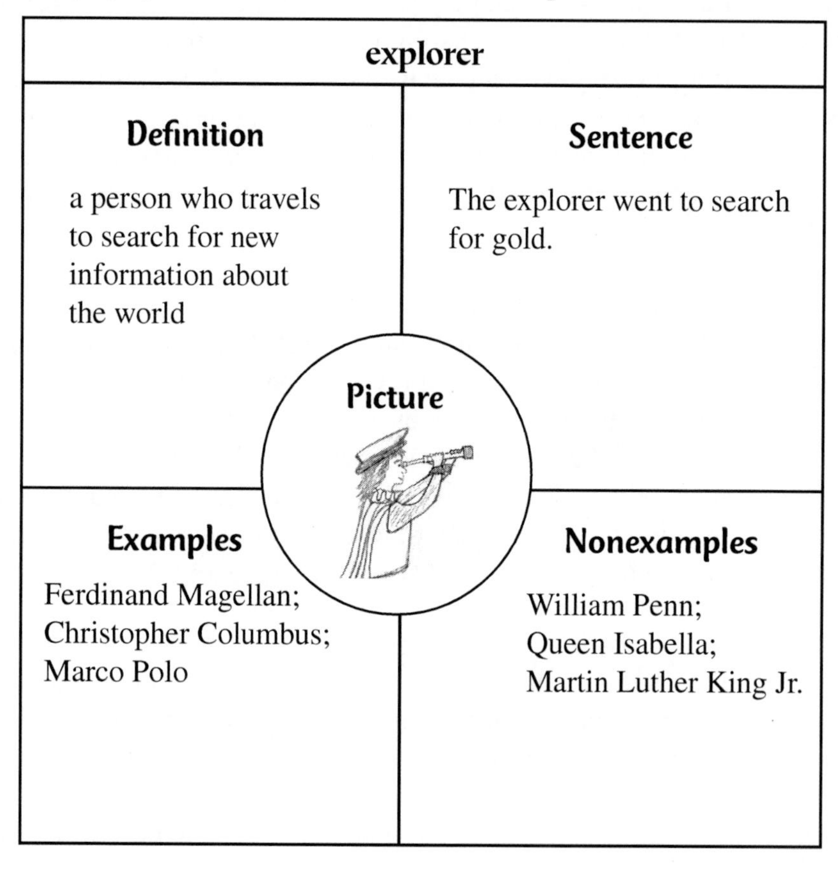

This encounter with new vocabulary enables students to use it properly. The definition identifies the word's meaning in student-friendly language. The sentence should be written so that the word is used in context. This helps the student make connections with background knowledge. Illustrating the sentence gives a visual clue. Examples help students prepare for factual questions from the teacher or on standardized assessments. Nonexamples help students prepare for ***not*** and ***except for*** test questions such as "All of these are explorers *except for* . . ." and "Which of these people is *not* an explorer?" Any information the student was unable to record before reading can be added after reading the text.

Strategies for Using the Leveled Texts *(cont.)*

Below-Grade-Level Students *(cont.)*

Graphic Organizers to Find Similarities and Differences

Setting a purpose for reading content focuses the learner. One purpose for reading can be to identify similarities and differences. This is a skill that must be directly taught, modeled, and applied. The authors of *Classroom Instruction That Works* state that identifying similarities and differences "might be considered the core of all learning" (Marzano, Pickering, and Pollock 2001, 14). Higher-level tasks include comparing and classifying information and using metaphors and analogies. One way to scaffold these skills is through the use of graphic organizers, which help students focus on the essential information and organize their thoughts.

Example Classifying Graphic Organizer

Explorer	Country sailed from	Land sailed to	Problems	Successes
Leif Eriksson	Scandinavia	Newfoundland	colony failed	discovered Vinland
Christopher Columbus	Spain	San Salvador	didn't reach Japan	returned a hero
Amerigo Vespucci	Italy	South America		America is named after him
Ferdinand Magellan	Spain	South America, Philippines	died while exploring	found a way around South America

The Riddles Graphic Organizer allows students to compare and contrast the explorers using riddles. Students first complete a chart you've designed. Then, using that chart, they can write summary sentences. They do this by using the riddle clues and reading across the chart. Students can also read down the chart and write summary sentences. With the chart below, students could write the following sentences: *Erikkson and Columbus sailed before 1500. Vespucci and Magellan sailed after 1500.*

Example Riddles Graphic Organizer

Who am I?	Eriksson	Columbus	Vespucci	Magellan
I sailed before 1500.	x	x		
I sailed in 1500 or later.			x	x
I sailed for Spain.		x		x
I died while exploring.				x
America is named after me.			x	

Strategies for Using the Leveled Texts *(cont.)*

Below-Grade-Level Students *(cont.)*

Framed Outline

This is an underused technique that bears great results. Many below-grade-level students have problems with reading comprehension. They need a framework to help them attack the text and gain confidence in comprehending the material. Once students gain confidence and learn how to locate factual information, the teacher can fade out this technique.

There are two steps to successfully using this technique. First, the teacher writes cloze sentences. Second, the students complete the cloze activity and write summary sentences.

Example Framed Outline

Around 986, the _________ sailed from Scandinavia. They crossed the ________ and landed in North America. When they came home, they told Leif _________. He wanted to ________ the new land. He set sail and landed in what is now ___________, Canada. Eriksson called the place ___________. It had many grapevines. But things went ________ and they did not stay.

Summary sentences: *Leif Eriksson sailed from Scandinavia to explore the new land. He discovered Vinland. But, things went wrong so the Vikings left.*

Modeling Written Responses

A frequent criticism heard by educators is that below-grade-level students write poor responses to content-area questions. This problem can be remedied if resource and classroom teachers model what good answers look like. While this may seem like common sense, few teachers take the time to do this. They just assume all children know how to respond in writing.

So, this is a technique you may want to use before asking your students to respond to the comprehension questions associated with the leveled texts in this series. First, read the question aloud. Then, write the question on an overhead and talk aloud about how you would go about answering the question. Next, write the answer using a complete sentence that accurately answers the question. Repeat the procedure for several questions so that students make the connection that quality written responses are your expectation.

As a warm-up activity, post a variety of responses to a single question. Ask students to identify the strongest responses and tell why they are strong. Have students identify the weakest answers and tell why they are weak. Ask for volunteers to come to the overhead and rewrite the weak responses so that they are strong. By doing this simple process, you are helping students evaluate and strengthen their own written responses.

Strategies for Using the Leveled Texts *(cont.)*

English Language Learners

By Marcela von Vacano

Effective teaching for English language learners requires effective planning. In order to achieve success, teachers need to understand and use a conceptual framework to help them plan lessons and units. There are six major components to any framework. Each is described in more detail below.

1. **Select and Define Concepts and Language Objectives**—Before having students read one of the texts in this book, the teacher must first choose a social studies concept and language objective (reading, writing, listening, or speaking) appropriate for the grade level. Then, the next step is to clearly define the concept to be taught. This requires knowledge of the subject matter, alignment with local and state objectives, and careful formulation of a statement that defines the concept. This concept represents the overarching idea. The social studies concept should be written on a piece of paper and posted in a visible place in the classroom.

   By the definition of the concept, post a set of key language objectives. Based on the content and language objectives, select essential vocabulary from the text. The number of new words selected should be based on students' English language levels. Post these words on a word wall that may be arranged alphabetically or by themes.

2. **Build Background Knowledge**—Some English language learners may have a lot of knowledge in their native language, while others may have little or no knowledge. The teacher will want to build the background knowledge of the students using different strategies such as the following:

   Visuals—Use posters, photographs, postcards, newspapers, magazines, drawings, and video clips of the topic you are presenting. The texts in this series include multiple primary sources for your use.

   Realia—Bring real-life objects to the classroom. If you are teaching about colonial times, bring in items such as a replica of a hornbook, a bonnet, or a tri-corner hat.

   Vocabulary and Word Wall—Introduce key vocabulary in context. Create families of words. Have students draw pictures that illustrate the words and write sentences about the words. Also be sure you have posted the words on a word wall in your classroom.

   Desk Dictionaries—Have students create their own desk dictionaries using index cards. On one side, they should draw a picture of the word. On the opposite side, they should write the word in their own language and in English.

Strategies for Using the Leveled Texts *(cont.)*

English Language Learners *(cont.)*

3. **Teach Concepts and Language Objectives**—The teacher must present content and language objectives clearly. He or she must engage students using a hook and must pace the delivery of instruction, taking into consideration the students' English language levels. The concept or concepts to be taught must be stated clearly. Use the first languages of the students whenever possible or assign other students who speak the same languages to mentor and to work cooperatively with the English language learners.

   Lev Semenovich Vygotsky, a Russian psychologist, wrote about the Zone of Proximal Development (ZPD). This theory states that good instruction must fill the gap that exists between the present knowledge of a child and the child's potential. Scaffolding instruction is an important component when planning and teaching lessons. English language learners cannot jump stages of language and content development. You must determine where the students are in the learning process and teach to the next level using several small steps to get to the desired outcome. With the leveled texts in this series and periodic assessment of students' language levels, teachers can support students as they climb the academic ladder.

4. **Practice Concepts and Language Objectives**—English language learners need to practice what they learn with engaging activities. Most people retain knowledge best after applying what they learn to their own lives. This is definitely true for English language learners. Students can apply content and language knowledge by creating projects, stories, skits, poems, or artifacts that show what they learned. Some activities should be geared to the right side of the brain, like those listed above. For students who are left-brain dominant, activities such as defining words and concepts, using graphic organizers, and explaining procedures should be developed. The following teaching strategies are effective in helping students practice both language and content:

   Simulations—Students recreate history by becoming a part of it. They have to make decisions as if they lived in historical times. For example, students can pretend that they are European explorers. They have to figure out what they would pack for an exploration trip. First, they need to brainstorm ideas, and then they can get the actual objects and put them in a small bag. Lastly, they present their objects to the class and give explanations for why they chose each item.

Strategies for Using the Leveled Texts *(cont.)*

English Language Learners *(cont.)*

4. **Practice Concepts and Language Objectives** *(cont.)*

    Literature response—Read a text from this book. Have students choose two people described or introduced in the text. Ask students to create a conversation the people might have. Or, you can have students write journal entries about events in the daily lives of the historic people.

    Have a short debate—Make a controversial statement such as, "*Slavery was necessary in the South.*" After reading a text in this book, have students think about the question and take a position. As students present their ideas, one student can act as a moderator.

    Interview—Students may interview a member of the family or a neighbor in order to obtain information regarding a topic from the texts in this book. For example: *How is your life similar to the lives of the early colonial settlers?*

5. **Evaluation and Alternative Assessments**—We know that evaluation is used to inform instruction. Students must have the opportunity to show their understanding of concepts in different ways and not only through standard assessments. Use both formative and summative assessment to ensure that you are effectively meeting your content and language objectives. Formative assessment is used to plan effective lessons for a particular group of students. Summative assessment is used to find out how much the students have learned. Other authentic assessments that show day-to-day progress are: text retelling, teacher rating scales, students self-evaluations, cloze testing, holistic scoring of writing samples, performance assessments, and portfolios. Periodically assessing student learning will help you ensure that students continue to receive the correct levels of texts.

6. **Home-School Connection**—The home-school connection is an important component in the learning process for English language learners. Parents are the first teachers, and they establish expectations for their children. These expectations help shape the behavior of their children. By asking parents to be active participants in the education of their children, students get a double dose of support and encouragement. As a result, families become partners in the education of their children and chances for success in your classroom increase.

    You can send home copies of the texts in this series for parents to read with their children. You can even send multiple levels to meet the needs of your second language parents as well as your students. In this way, you are sharing your social studies content standards with your whole second language community.

Strategies for Using the Leveled Texts *(cont.)*

Above-Grade-Level Students

By Wendy Conklin

Open-Ended Questions and Activities

Teachers need to be aware of activities that provide a ceiling that is too low for gifted students. When given activities like this, gifted students become bored. We know these students can do more, but how much more? Offering open-ended questions and activities will give high-ability students the opportunities to perform at or above their ability levels. For example, ask students to evaluate major events described in the texts, such as: "Do you think the colonists did the right thing by having the Boston Tea Party?" or "Did the king of Great Britain have the right to tax the colonists?" These questions require students to form opinions, think deeply about the issues, and form pro and con statements in their minds. To questions like this, there really is not one right answer.

The generic, open-ended question stems listed below can be adapted to any topic. There is one leveled comprehension question for each text in this book. The question stems below can be used to develop further comprehension questions for the leveled texts.

- In what ways did . . .
- How might you have done this differently . . .
- What if . . .
- What are some possible explanations for . . .
- How does this affect . . .
- Explain several reasons why . . .
- What problems does this create . . .
- Describe the ways . . .
- What is the best . . .
- What is the worst . . .
- What is the likelihood . . .
- Predict the outcome . . .
- Form a hypothesis . . .
- What are three ways to classify . . .
- Support your reason . . .
- Compare this to modern times . . .
- Make a plan for . . .
- Propose a solution . . .
- What is an alternative to . . .

Strategies for Using the Leveled Texts *(cont.)*

Above-Grade-Level Students *(cont.)*

Student-Directed Learning

Because they are academically advanced, gifted students are often the leaders in classrooms. They are more self-sufficient learners, too. As a result, there are some student-directed strategies that teachers can employ successfully with these students. Remember to use the texts in this book as jumpstarts so that students will be interested in finding out more about the time periods. Gifted students may enjoy any of the following activities:

- Writing their own questions, exchanging their questions with others, and grading the responses.
- Reviewing the lesson and teaching the topic to another group of students.
- Reading other nonfiction texts about this time period to further expand their knowledge.
- Writing the quizzes and tests to go along with the texts.
- Creating illustrated time lines to be displayed as visuals for the entire class.
- Putting together multimedia presentations using primary sources from the time period.
- Leading discussion groups about the texts or time periods.
- Researching topics from the texts in depth and writing new texts on these topics.

Tiered Assignments

Teachers can differentiate lessons by using tiered assignments, or scaffolded lessons. Tiered assignments are parallel tasks designed to have varied levels of depth, complexity, and abstractness. All students work toward one goal, concept, or outcome, but the lesson is tiered to allow for different levels of readiness and performance levels. As students work, they build on their prior knowledge and understanding. Students are motivated to be successful according to their own readiness and learning preferences.

Guidelines for writing tiered lessons include the following:

1. Pick the skill, concept, or generalization that needs to be learned.
2. Think of an on-grade-level activity that teaches this skill, concept, or generalization.
3. Assess the students using classroom discussions, quizzes, tests, or journal entries and place them in groups.
4. Take another look at the activity from Step 2. Modify this activity to meet the needs of the below-grade-level and above-grade-level learners in the class. Add complexity and depth for the above-grade-level learners . Add vocabulary support and concrete examples for the below-grade-level students.

How to Use This Product

Readability Chart

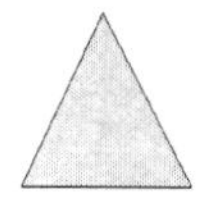

Title of the Text	Star	Circle	Square	Triangle
Exploring the New World	1.7	3.2	5.2	6.8
Explorers	1.5	3.1	5.1	6.9
American Indian Tribes of the East	1.7	3.2	5.0	7.0
American Indian Tribes of the Plains	1.8	3.1	5.0	6.9
American Indian Tribes of the West	1.7	3.1	5.1	7.0
The New England Colonies	2.0	3.4	5.2	7.1
The Middle Colonies	1.9	3.3	5.1	6.7
The Southern Colonies	1.6	3.5	5.1	6.8
Slavery in the New World	1.8	3.3	5.0	7.0
Causes of the American Revolution	1.9	3.2	5.1	6.9
The American Revolution	2.2	3.3	5.0	6.9
The Declaration of Independence	1.6	3.0	4.9	6.8
Early Congresses	1.9	3.1	5.0	7.0
The Constitution of the United States	2.1	3.3	4.9	6.5
The Bill of Rights	2.1	3.3	5.0	7.1

Correlation to Standards

The No Child Left Behind (NCLB) legislation mandates that all states adopt academic standards that identify the skills students will learn in kindergarten through grade 12. While many states had already adopted academic standards prior to NCLB, the legislation set requirements to ensure the standards were detailed and comprehensive. In many states today, teachers are required to demonstrate how their lessons meet state standards. State standards are used in the development of Shell Education products, so educators can be assured that they meet the academic requirements of each state.

Shell Education is committed to producing educational materials that are research and standards based. In this effort, all products are correlated to the academic standards of the 50 states, the District of Columbia, and the Department of Defense Dependent Schools. A correlation report customized for your state can be printed directly from the following website: **http://www.shelleducation.com**. If you require assistance in printing correlation reports, please contact Customer Service at 1-877-777-3450.

McREL Compendium

Shell Education uses the Mid-continent Research for Education and Learning (McREL) Compendium to create standards correlations. Each year, McREL analyzes state standards and revises the compendium. By following this procedure, they are able to produce a general compilation of national standards. The social studies standards on which the texts in this book focus are correlated to state standards at **http://www.shelleducation.com**.

How to Use This Product *(cont.)*

Components of the Product

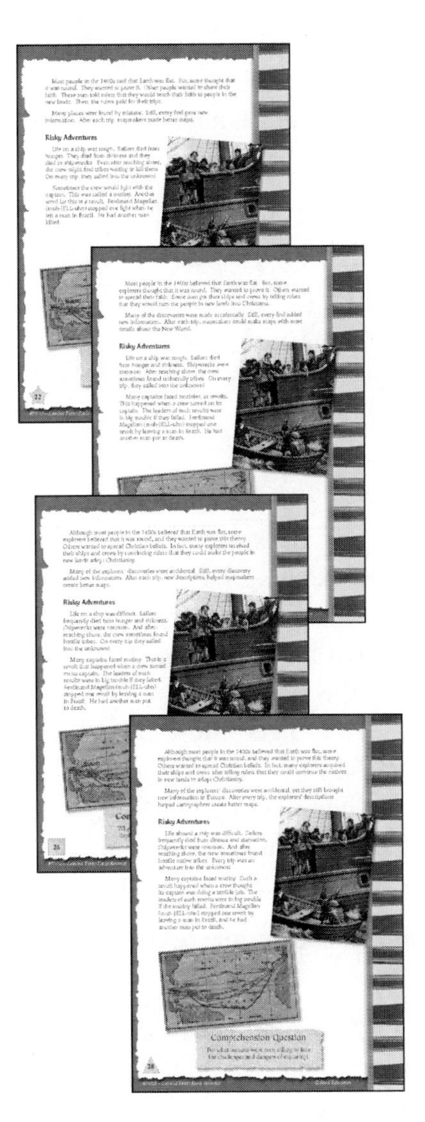

Primary Sources

- Each level of text includes multiple primary sources. These documents, photographs, and illustrations add interest to the texts. The historical images also serve as visual support for English language learners. They make the texts more context rich and bring the texts to life.

Comprehension Questions

- Each level of text includes one comprehension question. Like the texts, the comprehension questions were leveled by an expert. They are written to allow all students to be successful within a whole-class discussion. The questions for the same topic are closely linked so that the teacher can ask a question on that topic and all students will be able to answer. The lowest-level students might focus on the facts, while the upper-level students can delve deeper into the meanings.
- Teachers may want to base their whole-class question on the square level questions. Those were the starting points for all the other leveled questions.

The Levels

- There are 15 topics in this book. Each topic is leveled to four different reading levels. The images and fonts used for each level within a topic look the same.
- Behind each page number, you'll see a shape. These shapes indicate the reading levels of each piece so that you can make sure students are working with the correct texts. The reading levels fall into the ranges indicated to the left. See the chart on page 18 for specific levels of each text.

Levels 1.5–2.2

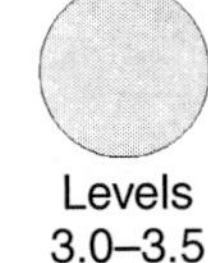
Levels 3.0–3.5

Levels 4.5–5.2

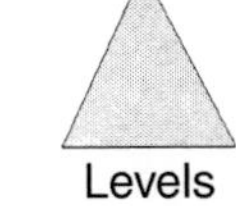
Levels 6.5–7.2

Leveling Process

- The texts in this series are taken from the Primary Source Readers kits published by Teacher Created Materials. A reading expert went through the texts and leveled each one to create four distinct reading levels.
- After that, a special education expert and an English language learner expert carefully reviewed the lowest two levels and suggested changes that would help their students comprehend the texts better.
- The texts were then leveled one final time to ensure the editorial changes made during the process kept them within the ranges described to the left.

How to Use This Product *(cont.)*

Tips for Managing the Product

How to Prepare the Texts

- When you copy these texts, be sure you set your copier to copy photographs. Run a few test pages and adjust the contrast as necessary. If you want the students to be able to appreciate the images, you need to carefully prepare the texts for them.
- You also have full-color versions of the texts provided in PDF form on the CD. (See page 144 for more information.) Depending on how many copies you need to make, printing the full-color versions and copying those might work best for you.
- Keep in mind that you should copy two-sided to two-sided if you pull the pages out of the book. The shapes behind the page numbers will help you keep the pages organized as you prepare them.

Distributing the Texts

- Some teachers wonder about how to hand the texts out within one classroom. They worry that students will feel insulted if they do not get the same papers as their neighbors. The first step in dealing with these texts is to set up your classroom as a place where all students learn at their individual instructional levels. Making this clear as a fact of life in your classroom is key. Otherwise, the students may constantly ask about why their work is different. You do not need to get into the technicalities of the reading levels. Just state it as a fact that every student will not be working on the same assignment every day. If you do this, then passing out the varied levels is not a problem. Just pass them to the correct students as you circle the room.
- If you would rather not have students openly aware of the differences in the texts, you can try these ways to pass out the materials.
    - Make a pile in your hands from star to triangle. Put your finger between the circle and square levels. As you approach each student, you pull from the top (star), above your finger (circle), below your finger (square), or the bottom (triangle). If you do not hesitate too much in front of each desk, the students will probably not notice.
    - Begin the class period with an opening activity. Put the texts in different places around the room. As students work quietly, circulate and direct students to the right locations for retrieving the texts you want them to use.
    - Organize the texts in small piles by seating arrangement so that when you arrive at a group of desks you have just the levels you need.

Exploring the New World

A Spicy Tale

There was a man named Marco Polo. He lived in Italy. He traveled to China. There, he saw many new things. In 1271, he wrote a book. This book had stories about the things he saw there. This made other people living in Europe want to explore, too.

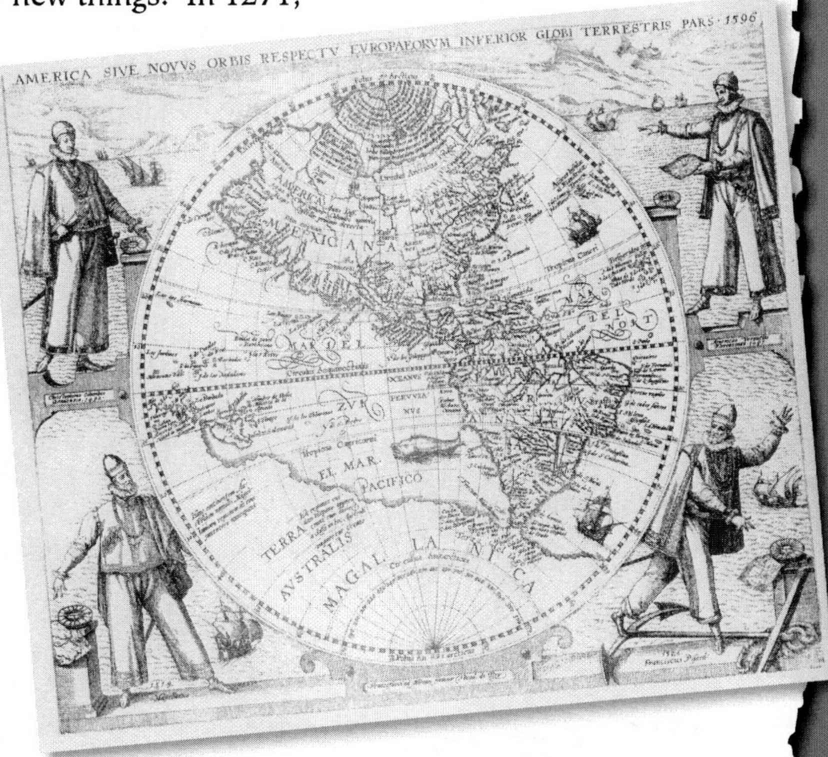

The people of Europe liked Asian spices. Their food often went bad. Spices could cover up the bad taste. Men hoped to find a way to go to the East by sea. They wanted to bring back spices on ships. Instead, sailors found land in the West. The world would never be the same.

The Lure to Explore

Explorers took risks because they wanted to be rich. They often died. Some people thought that they would find gold. Rulers wanted gold, too. Kings and queens paid for most of the trips. They thought that the men would bring back gold.

Most people in the 1400s said that Earth was flat. But, some thought that it was round. They wanted to prove it. Other people wanted to share their faith. These men told rulers that they would teach their faith to people in the new lands. Then, the rulers paid for their trips.

Many places were found by mistake. Still, every find gave new information. After each trip, mapmakers made better maps.

Risky Adventures

Life on a ship was rough. Sailors died from hunger. They died from sickness and they died in shipwrecks. Even after reaching shore, the crew might find tribes waiting to kill them. On every trip, they sailed into the unknown!

Sometimes the crew would fight with the captain. This was called a mutiny. Another word for this is a revolt. Ferdinand Magellan (muh-JELL-uhn) stopped one fight when he left a man in Brazil. He had another man killed.

Comprehension Question

What was hard about being an explorer?

Exploring the New World

A Spicy Tale

There was a man named Marco Polo who lived in Italy. He traveled to China and saw many new things. He wrote a book in the year 1271. It had stories about the things that he had seen there. This made other Europeans (yur-uh-PEE-uhns) interested in exploration.

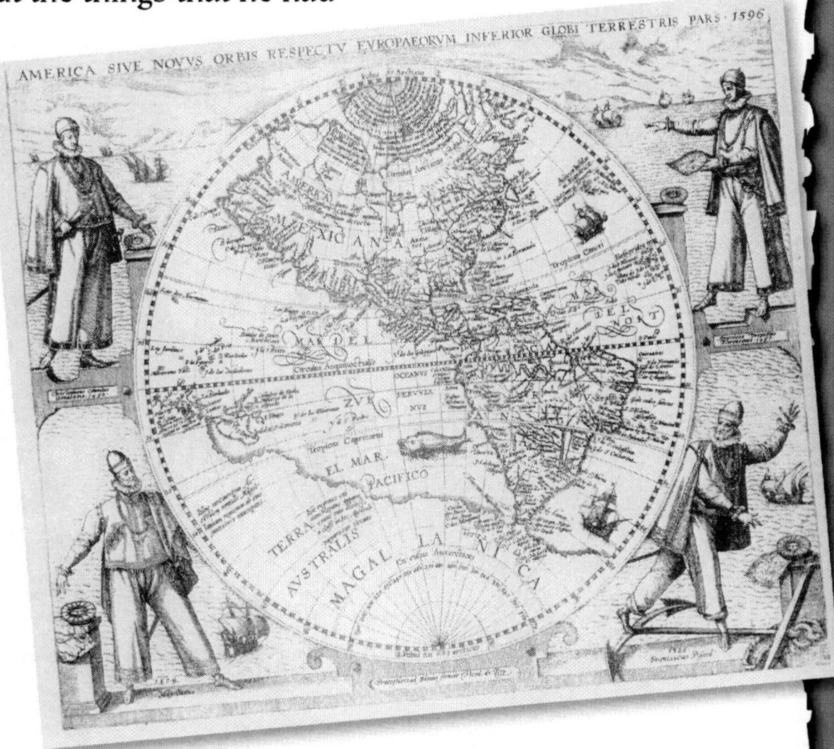

Europeans liked Asian spices. They had no way to keep food from spoiling. Spices covered up the bad taste. Merchants hoped to find a sea route to the East. They thought that it would be cheaper to move spices by ship than by land. While looking for a new sea route to Asia, explorers found land in the West. They had no idea how much this would change the world.

The Lure to Explore

Being an explorer meant risking death. Greed, science, and religion made men willing to take the risk. Some people thought that they would find gold in the New World. Kings and queens wanted gold, too. Rulers paid for most of the trips because they thought that their men would bring back lots of gold.

Most people in the 1400s believed that Earth was flat. But, some explorers thought that it was round. They wanted to prove it. Others wanted to spread their faith. Some men got their ships and crews by telling rulers that they would turn the people in new lands into Christians.

Many of the discoveries were made accidentally. Still, every find added new information. After each trip, mapmakers could make maps with more details about the New World.

Risky Adventures

Life on a ship was rough. Sailors died from hunger and sickness. Shipwrecks were common. After reaching shore, the crew sometimes found unfriendly tribes. On every trip, they sailed into the unknown!

Many captains faced mutinies, or revolts. This happened when a crew turned on its captain. The leaders of such revolts were in big trouble if they failed. Ferdinand Magellan (muh-JELL-uhn) stopped one revolt by leaving a man in Brazil. He had another man put to death.

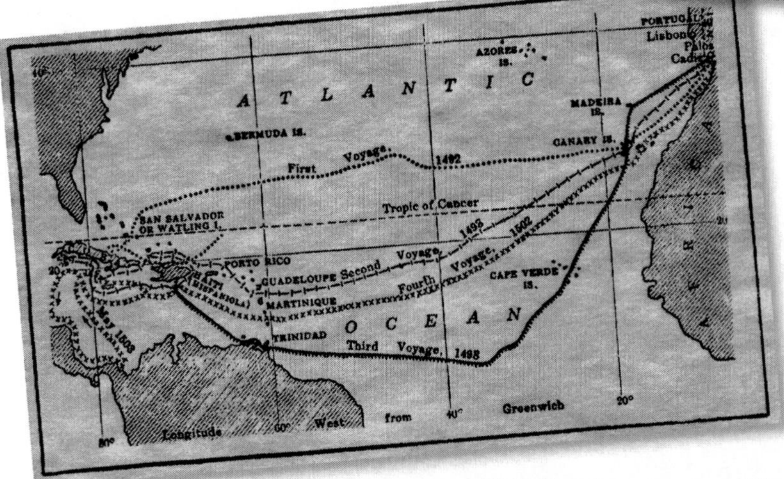

Comprehension Question

What are at least three things that made exploring hard?

Exploring the New World

A Spicy Tale

The Europeans' (yur-uh-PEE-uhns) quest for adventure began after Marco Polo returned from China. He wrote a book in the year 1271 filled with stories about the amazing things that he had seen there. This sparked others' imaginations and made them interested in exploration.

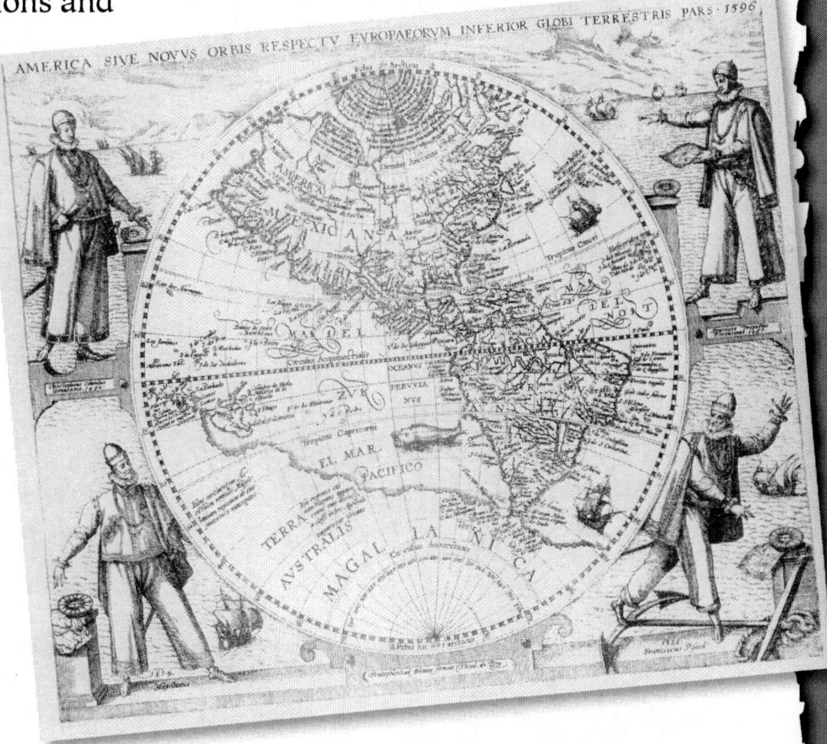

Europeans liked the taste of Asian spices. They had no way to keep their food from spoiling, and spices covered up the bad taste. Merchants wanted to find a sea route to the East. They thought that it would be cheaper to move spices by ship than by land. While seeking new sea routes to Asia, explorers found land in the West. They had no idea how much this would change the world.

The Lure to Explore

Being an explorer meant risking death. Greed, science, and religion made men willing to take such a risk. Some explorers thought they would find gold in the New World. The thought of such treasures also tempted kings and queens. Rulers funded most of the trips because they believed that large amounts of gold were located in faraway places.

Although most people in the 1400s believed that Earth was flat, some explorers believed that it was round, and they wanted to prove this theory. Others wanted to spread Christian beliefs. In fact, many explorers received their ships and crews by convincing rulers that they could make the people in new lands adopt Christianity.

Many of the explorers' discoveries were accidental. Still, every discovery added new information. After each trip, new descriptions helped mapmakers create better maps.

Risky Adventures

Life on a ship was difficult. Sailors frequently died from hunger and sickness. Shipwrecks were common. And after reaching shore, the crew sometimes found hostile tribes. On every trip they sailed into the unknown!

Many captains faced mutiny. This is a revolt that happened when a crew turned on its captain. The leaders of such revolts were in big trouble if they failed. Ferdinand Magellan (muh-JELL-uhn) stopped one revolt by leaving a man in Brazil. He had another man put to death.

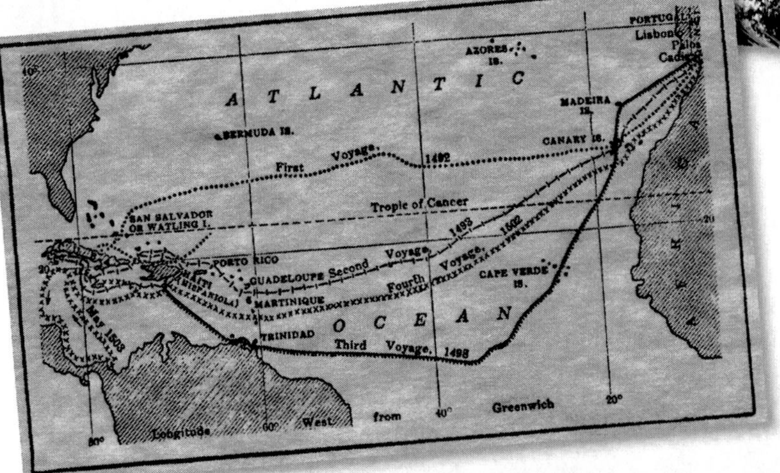

Comprehension Question

Why did men risk their lives to explore? Explain in detail at least three reasons.

Exploring the New World

A Spicy Tale

The Europeans' (yur-uh-PEE-uhns) quest for adventure began after Marco Polo wrote a book in the year 1271. His stories about his trip to China and the amazing things that he had seen there inspired others and generated great interest in exploration. Christopher Columbus even had a copy of Polo's book.

Europeans enjoyed the taste of Asian spices. They had no way to keep their food from spoiling, and spices helped to cover up the bad taste. Merchants wanted to find a sea route to the East because they believed it would be less expensive to transport spices by ship than by land. While seeking new sea routes to Asia, explorers accidentally discovered land in the West. None of them could imagine the impact these discoveries would have on the world.

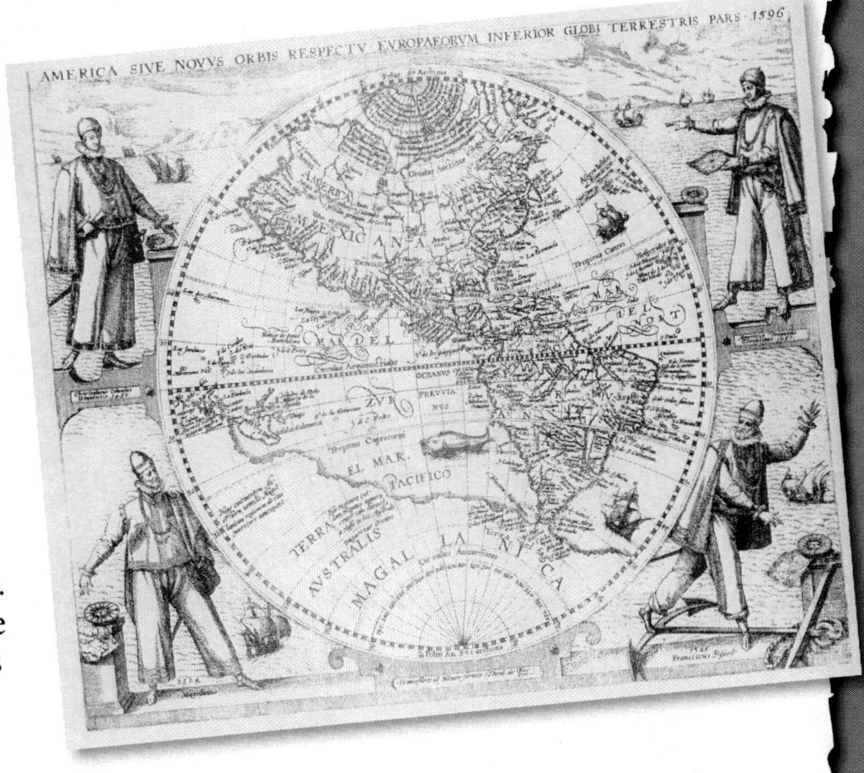

The Lure to Explore

Greed, science, and religion made men willing to risk their lives as explorers. Many dreamed of finding precious metals. The thought of such treasures tempted kings and queens as well. Believing that large amounts of gold were located in faraway places, rulers funded most of the trips.

27

Although most people in the 1400s believed that Earth was flat, some explorers thought that it was round, and they wanted to prove this theory. Others wanted to spread Christian beliefs. In fact, many explorers acquired their ships and crews after telling rulers that they could convince the natives in new lands to adopt Christianity.

Many of the explorers' discoveries were accidental, yet they still brought new information to Europe. After every trip, the explorers' descriptions helped cartographers create better maps.

Risky Adventures

Life aboard a ship was difficult. Sailors frequently died from disease and starvation. Shipwrecks were common. And after reaching shore, the crew sometimes found hostile native tribes. Every trip was an adventure into the unknown!

Many captains faced mutiny. Such a revolt happened when a crew thought its captain was doing a terrible job. The leaders of such revolts were in big trouble if the mutiny failed. Ferdinand Magellan (muh-JELL-uhn) stopped one revolt by leaving a man in Brazil, and he had another man put to death.

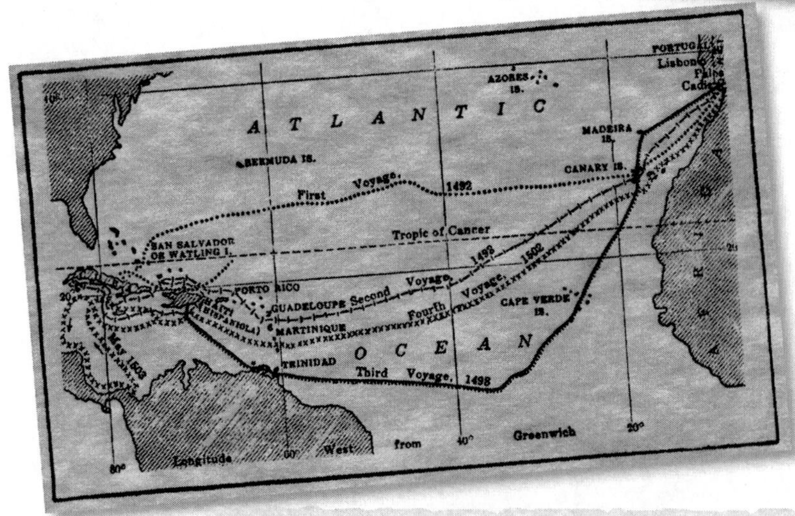

Comprehension Question

For what reasons were men willing to face the challenges and dangers of exploring?

Explorers

The Vikings in North America

The Vikings were sailors. They lived in Europe. The Vikings sailed across the ocean. In 986, they reached North America. Then, they went back home. They told a man named Leif Eriksson about their trip. He wanted to explore, too. So he set sail. He landed in what is now Canada. He named it Vinland. Why? It had lots of grapevines.

Some Vikings tried to settle in the new land. But things went wrong. So, they left.

Columbus and Vespucci Reach the Americas

Christopher Columbus was an explorer. He wanted to find a new sea route to China. King Ferdinand and Queen Isabella of Spain said they would help. They gave him sailors. They gave him three ships, too. The ships were named *Niña, Pinta,* and *Santa María*.

In August 1492, the ships left Spain. They sailed west across the Atlantic Ocean. On October 12, the sailors saw land. It was San Salvador. This is in the Bahamas. They went ashore. Christopher Columbus thought they were near Japan. He went home and became a hero.

Around 1500, Amerigo Vespucci (vess-POO-chee) went to the New World. He made four trips. He wrote about the people and the animals that he had seen. A mapmaker read his story. In 1507, this man made a map. He put the name America on it. America is named after Amerigo Vespucci.

The First Trip Around the World

Ships from Europe sailed south around the tip of Africa. That was how they went to Asia. But Ferdinand Magellan (muh-JELL-uhn) wanted a new route. He had five ships and 270 men. They sailed west from Spain. They found a strait. This is a narrow opening of water. It was near the tip of South America.

Then, Ferdinand Magellan told his crew the truth. They were sailing around the world! The crew almost ran out of food. They nearly died of hunger. At last, they reached some islands. It was the Philippines. There, they got food. But Magellan died in a fight. Just one of his ships and 18 men made it back to Spain.

Comprehension Question

Name the explorers who reached America first.

Explorers

The Vikings in North America

Around the year 986, the Vikings sailed from Scandinavia (scan-dih-NAY-vee-uh). They crossed the Atlantic Ocean and landed in North America. When they came home, they told Leif Eriksson. He wanted to explore the new land. He set sail and landed in what is now Newfoundland, Canada. Eriksson called the place Vinland because it had many grapevines.

The Vikings tried to settle in the new land. But things went wrong and they did not stay. There is proof of an old Viking settlement in Newfoundland.

Columbus and Vespucci Reach the Americas

Christopher Columbus wanted to find a new sea route to China. He asked King Ferdinand and Queen Isabella of Spain for their help. They gave him a crew and three ships. The ships' names were *Niña, Pinta,* and *Santa María.*

These ships left Spain in August 1492. They sailed west across the Atlantic Ocean. Christopher Columbus thought that he was heading to Japan. Instead, on October 12, the crew landed at San Salvador. This is located in what is now the Bahamas. But Columbus thought that they had reached an island near Japan. Columbus thought that he had succeeded. He went back as a hero.

Around 1500, Amerigo Vespucci (vess-POO-chee) explored the New World. He made four trips to South America. He wrote about the people and the odd animals that he saw. A mapmaker read Vespucci's writings. In 1507, the mapmaker made a map. He put the name America on the map. America is named after Amerigo Vespucci.

The First Trip Around the World

European ships had always sailed around the southern tip of Africa to reach Asia. Ferdinand Magellan (muh-JELL-uhn) wanted to find a new route. He sailed west from Spain. He had five ships and 270 men. He found a strait, or narrow waterway. It was near the southern tip of South America. Then, Magellan told his crew that they were sailing around the world! The crew almost died of hunger. At last they reached the Philippines. There, Magellan died in a fight with a tribe. Only one of his ships and 18 men made it back to Spain.

Comprehension Question

Which explorers reached the Americas first?

Explorers

The Vikings in North America

Around 986, the Vikings sailed from Scandinavia (scan-dih-NAY-vee-uh). They crossed the Atlantic Ocean and landed in North America. When they returned home, they told Leif Eriksson. He decided to explore this new land, and he followed the same course. He probably landed in Newfoundland, Canada. Eriksson called the place Vinland because of the many grapevines.

The Vikings tried to settle in the new land without success. Archaeologists (ar-key-OL-uh-jists) have found the remnants of an ancient Viking settlement in Newfoundland.

Columbus and Vespucci Reach the Americas

Christopher Columbus asked King Ferdinand and Queen Isabella of Spain to help him find a new sea passage to China. They gave him a crew and three ships—the *Niña, Pinta,* and *Santa María.*

These ships left Spain on August 2, 1492, and sailed west across the Atlantic Ocean. Columbus believed that he was following a line of latitude (lat-uh-TOOD) that would take him to Japan. Instead, on October 12, the crew landed at San Salvador. This is located in what is now the Bahamas. But Columbus thought that they had reached an island near Japan. Thinking that he had been successful, Columbus went home a hero.

Around 1500, Amerigo Vespucci (vess-POO-chee) explored the New World. He made four trips to South America. He wrote descriptions of the natives and the unusual animals that he saw. A cartographer read Vespucci's writings, and in 1507, he printed a map with the name America on the southern continent. America was named for Amerigo.

The First Trip Around the World

To reach Asia, European ships had always sailed around the southern tip of Africa. Ferdinand Magellan (muh-JELL-uhn) decided to find another route. He sailed west from Spain with five ships and 270 men. He found a narrow strait, or water passage, near South America's southern tip. Then, Magellan told his crew that they were really sailing around the world! The crew almost starved. Magellan died in a battle against a tribe in the Philippines. Only one of his ships and 18 men made it back to Spain.

Comprehension Question

Which European(s) should be given credit for first exploring the Americas?

Explorers

The Vikings in North America

Around 986, the Vikings sailed from Scandinavia (scan-dih-NAY-vee-uh) to North America. When these Vikings returned home, they told of their adventure. Leif Eriksson decided to explore this new land, and he followed the same course. He probably landed in Newfoundland, Canada. Eriksson called the place Vinland because of the many grapevines.

The Vikings attempted to settle in the new land without success. Archaeologists (ar-key-OL-uh-jists) have found the remnants of an ancient Viking settlement in Newfoundland.

Columbus and Vespucci Reach the Americas

Christopher Columbus asked King Ferdinand and Queen Isabella of Spain to help him sail to China. They provided him with a crew and three ships—the *Niña*, *Pinta*, and *Santa María*.

These ships left Spain on August 2, 1492, and headed west across the Atlantic Ocean. Columbus believed that he was following a line of latitude (lat-uh-TOOD) that would take him to Japan. But instead, on October 12, the crew landed at San Salvador in the Bahamas. Columbus mistakenly thought that they had reached an island near Japan. Believing that he had been successful, Columbus sailed home a hero.

The Italian Amerigo Vespucci (vess-POO-chee) explored the New World around 1500. Vespucci made four trips to South America and wrote descriptions of the natives and the unusual animals that he saw. Martin Waldseemüller (zalt-ZAY-mew-ler), a cartographer, read Vespucci's writings, and in 1507, he printed a map with the name America on the southern continent. America was his adaptation of Amerigo.

The First Trip Around the World

To reach Southeast Asia, European ships had always sailed around the southern tip of Africa. Ferdinand Magellan (muh-JELL-uhn) decided to find an alternate route. He sailed west from Spain with five ships and 270 men. He discovered a narrow strait, or water passageway, near South America's southern tip. Then, Magellan announced to his crew that they were sailing around the world! The crew nearly starved before reaching the Philippines. Magellan died in a battle against a tribe in the Philippines. Only one of his ships and 18 men returned to Spain.

Comprehension Question

Explain why Christopher Columbus is the European given credit for discovering the Americas.

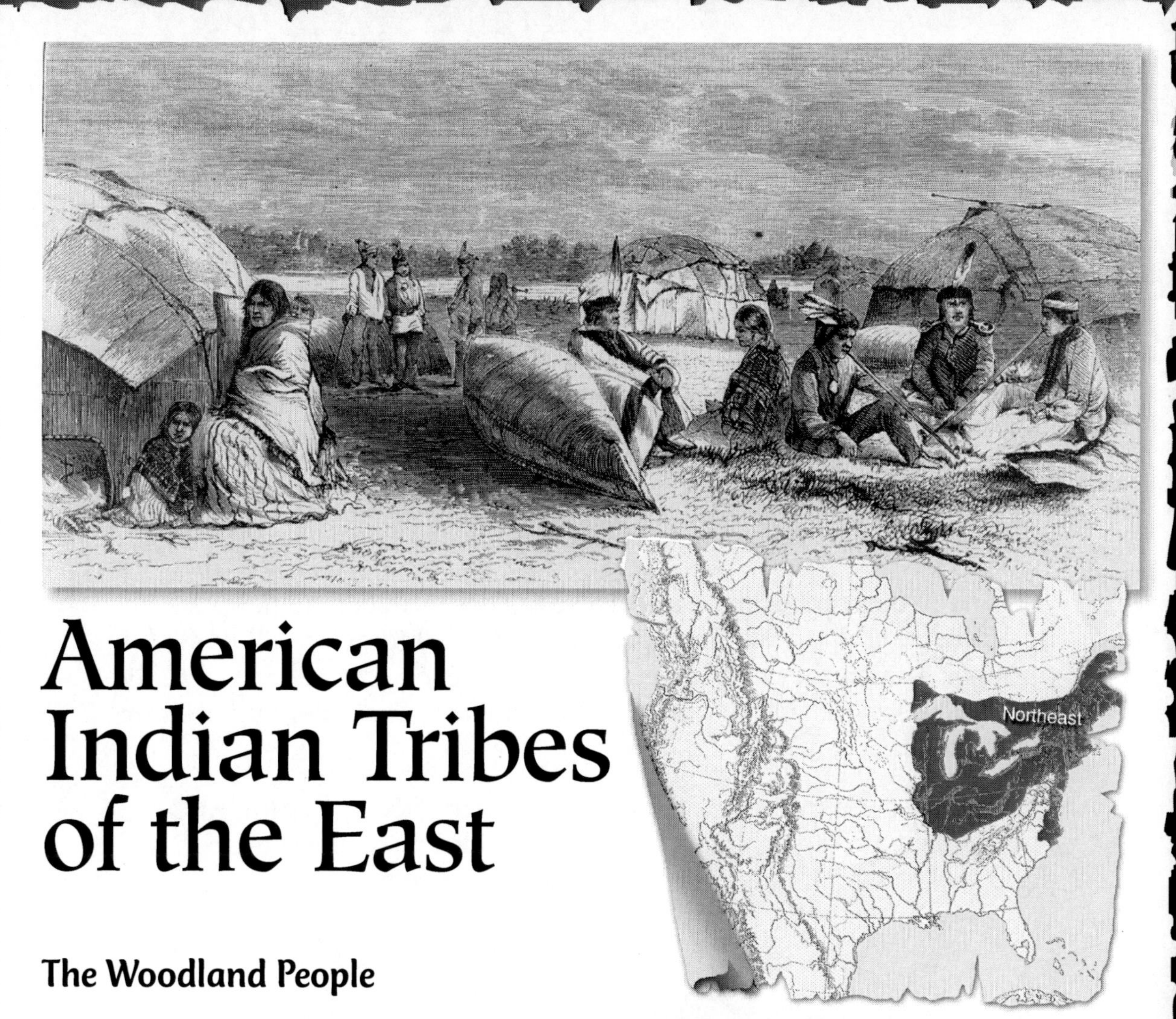

American Indian Tribes of the East

The Woodland People

Some American Indians lived in the Northeast of the United States. They were called the Woodland People. They had a lot of trees on their land. They made pots, tools, and canoes from wood. They put walls made of wooden posts around their towns. These walls were called palisades.

Most of the Indians lived in houses called wigwams. These were dome-shaped homes. Each one had a smoke hole in the top. The outside of the wigwam was covered with bark from trees. One family lived in each wigwam. Some tribes built long houses. These homes were made of poles and bark. They had rounded roofs. A few families lived in each long house.

These Indians planted crops. They grew corn, beans, squash, and yams. Corn was the most important crop. The people ate it. Then, they used the other parts of the corn to make bedding and shoes.

The American Indians loved nature. They thought that each thing had a spirit. When the tribe members ate an animal, they would say a prayer. They honored the spirits of things in other ways, too. The tribes held ceremonies (SER-uh-mo-neez).

The Southeastern Indians

The Southeast is another area in the United States. In southeastern tribes, mothers were very important. A person was related to other people only on the mother's side. When a couple got married, they lived with the woman's family. The tribes saw women as most important. Still, men made most of the choices.

Some of these tribes lived in chickees. These wooden homes were up off the ground. They were open on all sides. Breezes could blow through. The breezes helped keep the people cool. They lived where the summers were hot. Other tribes built log homes. These kept them warm in the winter.

The tribes had many jobs to do. The women took care of the gardens. They looked after the children. The women also made baskets and pottery. The men hunted deer, bear, and rabbits to eat.

Comprehension Question

Name at least two types of American Indian homes.

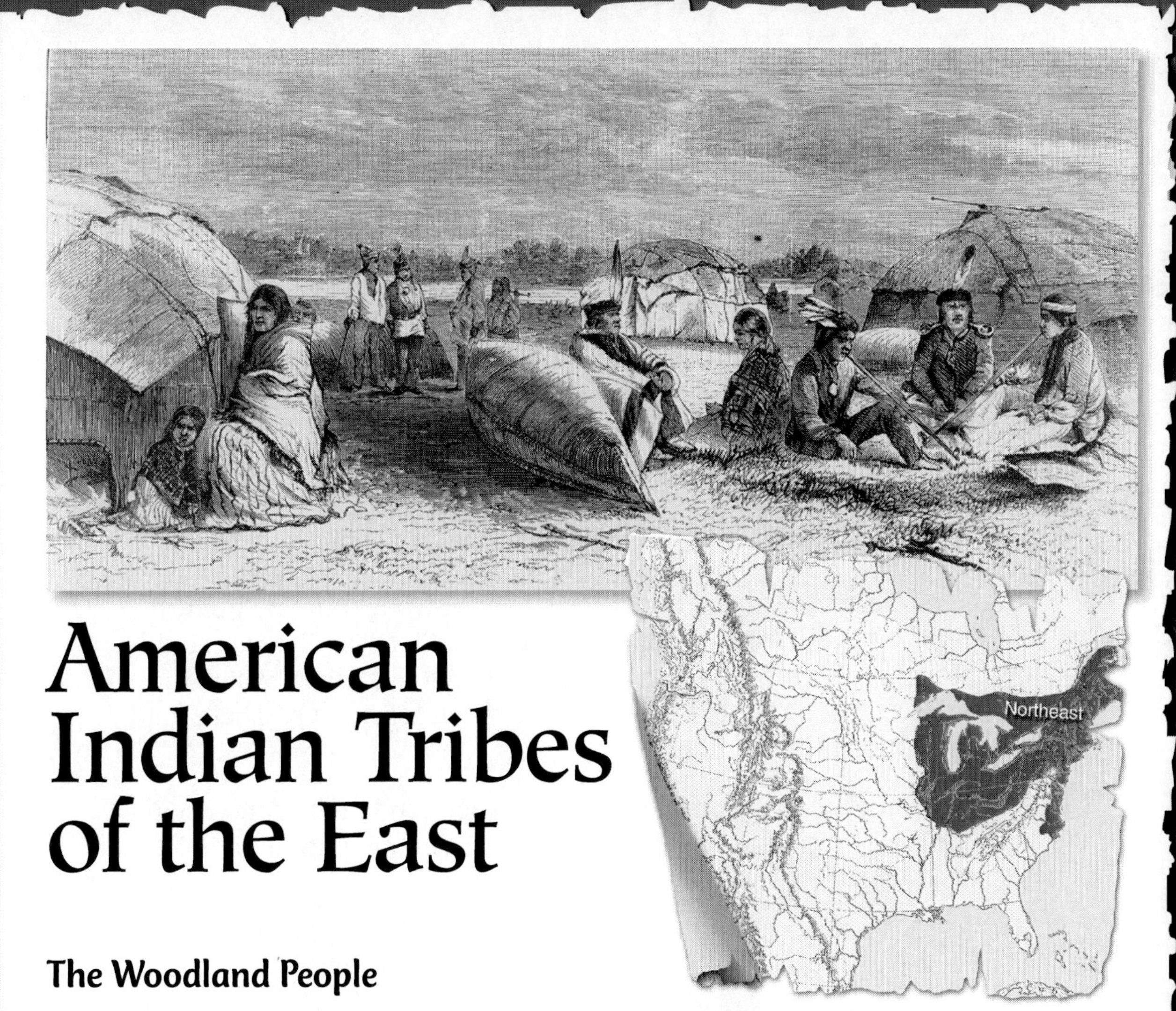

American Indian Tribes of the East

The Woodland People

The northeastern American Indian tribes were called the Woodland People. They had lots of trees on their land. So, they made dishes, pots, tools, and even canoes from wood. They built tall walls of sharp wooden posts around their villages, too. The walls were called palisades. Most tribes lived in wigwams. Wigwams were dome-shaped, bark-covered homes. Each one had a smoke hole in the top. One family lived in each wigwam. Some tribes lived in long houses. These long buildings were made of poles and bark. They had rounded roofs. A few families lived inside each one.

Many northeastern Indians planted crops. They grew corn, beans, squash, and yams. The most important crop was corn. The people ate the corn. Then, they used the cobs and husks to make crafts, bedding, and shoes.

The American Indians honored nature. They thought that everything had a spirit. After eating an animal, the tribe offered a prayer. They might also show respect by having a ceremony (SER-uh-mo-nee). Medicine men led the ceremonies.

The Southeastern Indians

In southeastern tribes, women were very important. These tribes were matrilineal (ma-truh-LIN-ee-uhl). People were related to each other through the women. When a couple married, they lived with the woman's family. The tribes respected women. Still, men made most of the decisions.

Some of these tribes lived in chickees. These wooden frame homes were raised off the ground. They were open on all sides. Breezes could blow through. This helped keep the people cool. They lived where the summers were hot and humid. Other tribes built log homes. These kept them warm in the winter.

Tribe members had specific jobs. The women tended the gardens and the children. They made baskets and pottery. The men hunted. They killed deer, bear, and rabbits for the tribe to eat.

Comprehension Question

Describe two kinds of American Indian homes.

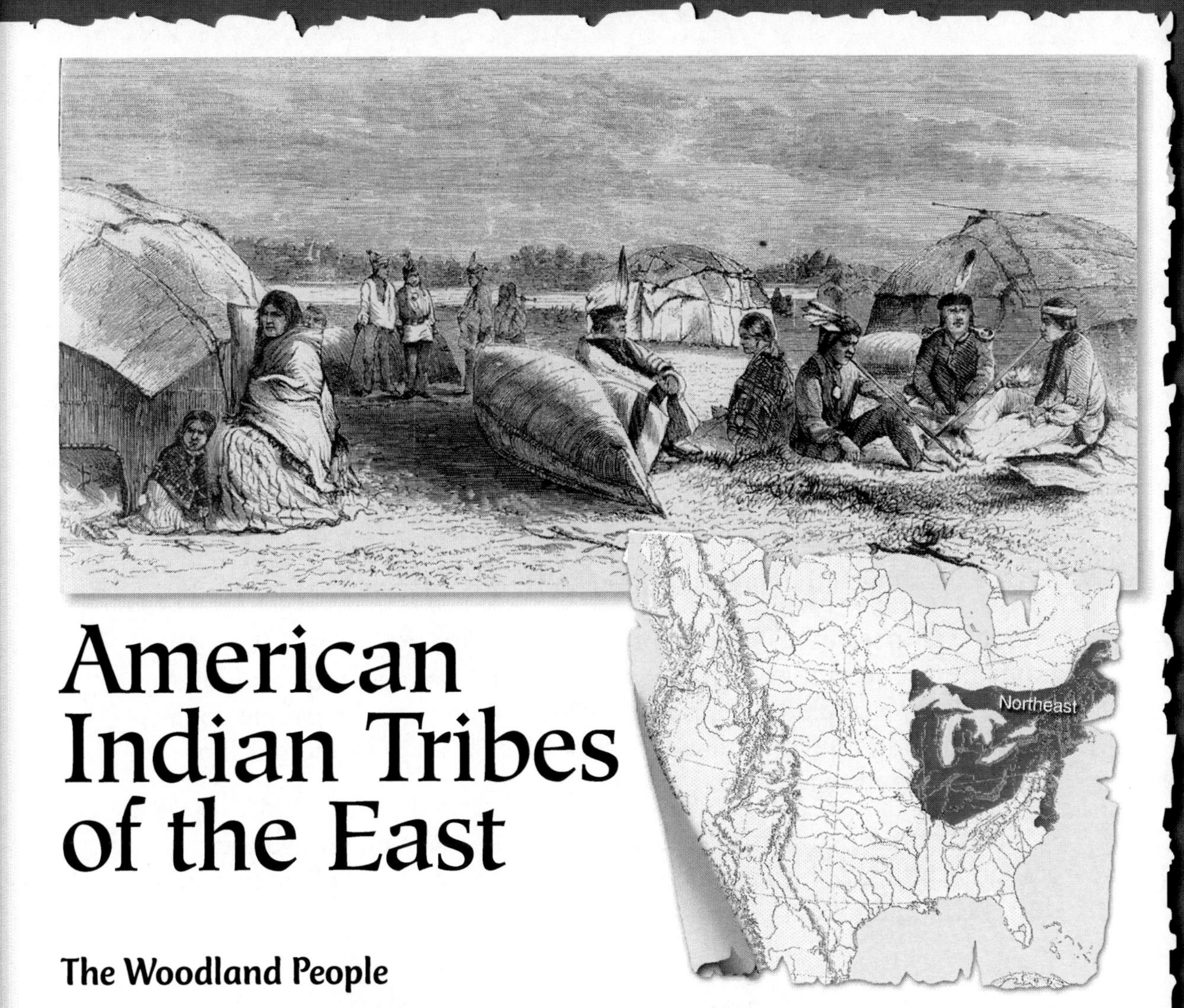

American Indian Tribes of the East

The Woodland People

The northeastern American Indian tribes were called the Woodland People. They had many trees in their region. So, they learned to make baskets, canoes, tools, pots, and dishes from wood. They surrounded their villages with tall walls. The walls were called palisades. These walls were made of sharp wooden posts. Most of the Indians lived in homes called wigwams that were just large enough for one family. Wigwams were dome-shaped, bark-covered houses. Each one had a smoke hole in the top. Some tribes lived in long houses made from bark and poles. These long buildings had rounded roofs. Several families lived together within each one.

Many northeastern Indians were farmers. They tended crops of corn, beans, squash, and yams. Their most important crop was corn. The people used every part of the corn. They ate the kernels and used the cobs and husks for crafts, bedding, shoes, and ceremonies (SER-uh-mo-neez).

These American Indians had a deep respect for nature and believed that everything had a spirit. Thus, after eating an animal, tribe members offered a prayer or a sacrifice (SAK-rih-fice). Another way they showed respect for spirits was to hold a special ceremony. This type of ceremony was led by a medicine man.

The Southeastern Indians

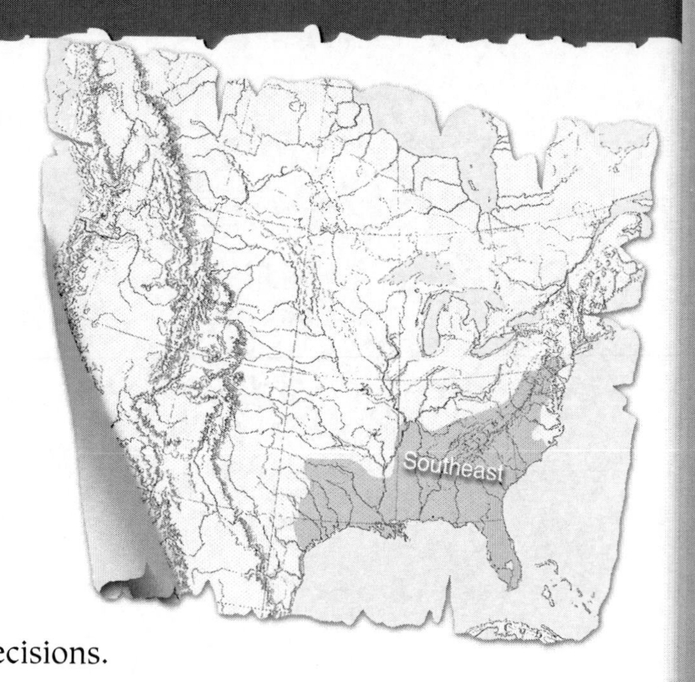

The southeastern tribes were matrilineal (ma-truh-LIN-ee-uhl). This means that an individual's relatives were all the people who were related to him or her on the mother's side of the family. When a young couple married, they lived with the woman's family. Women held places of honor within the tribes. Even so, the men made the important decisions.

Some of these tribes lived in homes called chickees. These wooden-frame homes were raised off the ground. They were open on all four sides. Breezes could blow through. This helped keep the people cool during the hot, humid summers. Other tribes lived in log homes that protected them from the cold of winter.

Members of the tribes had specific jobs. The women tended the gardens and made baskets, pottery, and silver jewelry, while men hunted deer, bear, and rabbits.

Comprehension Question

How did homes in the Northeast and Southeast differ?

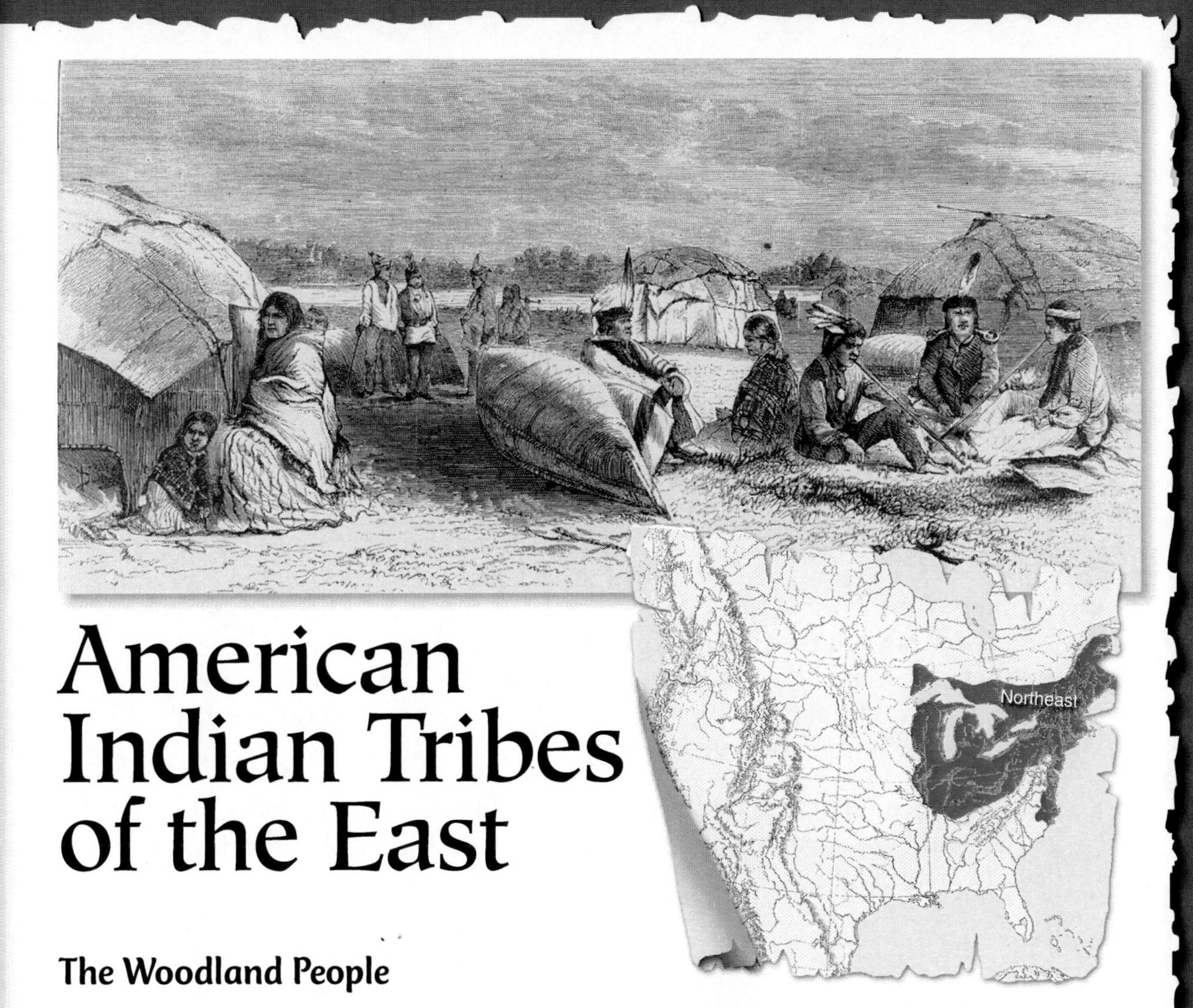

American Indian Tribes of the East

The Woodland People

The northeastern American Indian tribes were called the Woodland People. They excelled at making baskets, canoes, tools, pots, and dishes from wood. They surrounded their villages with tall palisades, which are walls made of sharp wooden posts. Most of the Indians lived in homes, called wigwams, that were only large enough for one family. A wigwam was a dome-shaped, bark-covered house with a smoke hole opening in the top. Some tribes lived in long houses made from bark and poles. These long buildings had rounded roofs and several families lived together within them.

Many northeastern Indians were farmers. They planted crops of corn, beans, squash, and yams. Their most important crop was corn. The people used every part of the corn, eating the kernels and using the cobs and husks for crafts, bedding, shoes, and ceremonies (SER-uh-mo-neez).

These American Indians had a deep respect for nature and believed that everything in nature had a spirit. Thus, after eating an animal, tribe members offered a prayer or a sacrifice (SAK-rih-fice). They might also show respect for the spirits by holding a special ceremony led by a medicine man.

The Southeastern Indians

The southeastern tribes were matrilineal (ma-truh-LIN-ee-uhl), which means that an individual's relatives were all the people who were related on the mother's side of the family. When a young couple married, they lived with the woman's family. Women held places of honor within the tribes, but even so, the men made the most important decisions.

Some of these tribes lived in homes called chickees. These wooden-frame homes were raised off the ground and open on all four sides so that breezes could blow through. This helped keep the Indians cool during the hot, humid summers. Other tribes lived in log homes that protected them from the cold of winter.

Members of the tribes had specific jobs. The women tended the gardens and made baskets, pottery, and silver jewelry, while men hunted deer, bear, and rabbits.

Comprehension Question

In what ways did the American Indian homes reflect the geography of the regions?

American Indian Tribes of the Plains

The Plains People

The middle of the country is very flat. The Indians who lived there were the Plains Indians. There were about 30 tribes. They lived in small groups. They did not make villages. This is why they could move quickly. They had to move often. They followed their food. And, they tried to stay away from their enemies.

Some of them lived in grass houses. Others lived in earth, or mud, houses. But, most of the Plains Indians lived in tepees. A tepee was like a tent. It was made with a bison skin and long poles. The skin was pulled over the poles. It formed a cone shape. The pole ends crossed. They stuck out at the top. Pegs held the tent down. Tepees were easy to pack, move, and set up.

Family was important to the Plains Indians. They believed a whole family should help raise the children. Grandparents, aunts, and uncles all helped parents.

The tribes played music and danced. The Sioux Sun Dance gave thanks to the Creator. This event lasted four days. Trees were hard to find. In the first three days, the people had to find and cut down a tree. Then, they put up a wooden pole. On the fourth day, young men danced around the pole.

The Bison Bunch

Bison lived on the plains. The Indians knew how to use every part of a bison. They ate the meat. They made their clothes and blankets from the skins. The bones of the bison were used to make tools, pots, and shields.

The Plains men hunted bison. They trained the horses. They also protected the tribe and made weapons. The Plains women gathered and cooked the food. They took care of the small children. They gave the older children chores to do. They also dried the bison skins and made necklaces of beads.

Comprehension Question

Why did the Plains Indians move so much?

American Indian Tribes of the Plains

The Plains People

The Plains Indians included about 30 tribes. They had to move often. They followed their food and tried to stay away from enemies. They lived in small groups. They did not build villages. This let them move quickly if needed.

Some of the Plains Indians lived in grass houses or earth lodges. But, most of them lived in tepees. A tepee is a kind of tent. A tepee is made by stretching a bison skin over long poles. The poles helped the skin to form a cone shape. The pole ends crossed. They stuck out at the top. Pegs held the tent to the ground. Tepees were used because they were easy to pack, move, and set up.

Wichita grass house

Dakota tepee

Mandan earth lodge

The Plains Indians thought that a whole family should raise the children. Grandparents, aunts, and uncles all helped parents with their children. If children's parents died, they were taken into other families.

The tribes' ceremonies had music and dancing. The Sioux Sun Dance was done to give thanks to the Creator. The Indians thought that this dance would make the Creator take care of their needs. The celebration lasted for four days. Trees were not common. In the first three days, the people had to find, cut, and put up a wooden sun dance pole. On the fourth day, young men danced around it.

The Bison Bunch

Many bison lived on the Plains. The Indians relied on them. The Indians knew how to make use of every part of a bison. They ate the meat. Then, they made the skins into clothing, blankets, and tepee covers. Tools, pots, and shields came from bison bones.

The Plains men hunted bison and trained the tribe's horses. They also protected the tribe and made weapons. The Plains women gathered and prepared the food. They took care of the small children and supervised the older children's chores. The women dried the bison skins and made necklaces from beads.

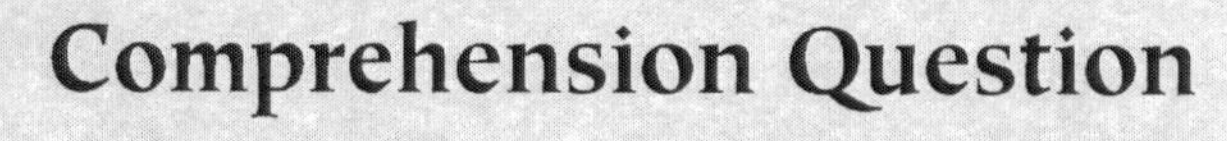

Comprehension Question

Why did the Plains Indians have to move quickly?

American Indian Tribes of the Plains

The Plains People

The Plains Indians included about 30 tribes. Their lifestyle included moving often to follow their food and to stay away from their enemies. They lived in small groups. This let them move quickly whenever the need arose. They did not establish permanent villages.

Some of the Plains Indians lived in grass houses or earth lodges. But most of them lived in tepees, which is a kind of tent. They made a tepee by stretching a bison skin over long poles. The poles helped the skin form a cone shape. The pole ends crossed and stuck out at the top. The tent was pegged to the ground at the base. Tepees were popular because they were easy to pack and set up.

Wichita grass house

Mandan earth lodge

Dakota tepee

The tribes on the Plains believed that the whole family should raise the children. Grandparents, aunts, and uncles all helped parents with their children. Orphaned children were welcomed into other families.

Music and dancing were important in the Plains tribal ceremonies (SER-uh-mo-neez). The Sioux Sun Dance was performed by the Indians to give thanks to the Creator, who lived in the sun. They believed that the Creator would provide for their needs because of this celebration, which lasted for four days. Trees were not common in the area. In the first three days, the ceremony was on finding, cutting, and creating a tall, straight tree called the sun dance pole. On the fourth day, young men danced around the pole.

The Bison Bunch

Thousands of bison lived on the Plains. This large animal helped the people to survive. The Indians knew how to make use of every part of a bison. They ate the meat and then made the skins into clothing, blankets, and tepee covers. Tools, needles, pots, and shields came from bison bones.

The Plains men hunted bison and trained the tribe's horses. They also protected the tribe, made weapons, and fought when necessary. The Plains women gathered and prepared the food. They took care of the small children and supervised the older children's chores. The women dried the bison skins and made beaded necklaces.

Comprehension Question

How did living in small groups help the Plains Indians survive?

American Indian Tribes of the Plains

The Plains People

The Plains Indians were comprised of approximately 30 large tribes. Their lifestyle included moving frequently in order to follow their food source and stay away from their enemies. As a result, they lived in small groups so they could move rapidly whenever the need arose. They did not establish permanent villages.

Some of the Plains Indians lived in grass houses or earth lodges, but the majority of them lived in tepees, which is a kind of tent. They created a tepee by stretching bison skin over long poles. The poles helped the skin to form a cone shape. The pole ends crossed and stuck out at the top. The tepee was pegged to the ground at the base. These shelters were popular because they were easy to quickly set up or pack.

The Plains Indians believed that the entire family should raise the children, so grandparents, aunts, and uncles all assisted parents with their children. Orphaned children were quickly welcomed into other families.

Music and dancing were essential elements of the Plains tribal ceremonies (SER-uh-mo-neez). The Sioux Sun Dance was performed by the Indians to offer gratitude to the Creator, who lived in the sun. They believed that the Creator would provide for their needs because of this celebration, which lasted for four days. Trees were uncommon in the area. So, for the first three days, the ceremony included finding, cutting, and erecting a tall, straight tree called the sun dance pole. On the fourth day, young men danced around the pole.

The Bison Bunch

Thousands of bison lived on the Plains, and the people there depended on them for survival. The Indians knew how to make use of every part of a bison. They ate the meat and then utilized the skins for clothing, blankets, and tepee covers. Tools, needles, pots, and shields came from bison bones.

The Plains men spent their time hunting bison, training the tribe's horses, protecting the tribe, making weapons, and going to war when necessary. The Plains women gathered and prepared the food, dried the bison skins, and made beaded necklaces. They took care of the young children and supervised the older children's daily chores.

Comprehension Question

In what ways was the tepee the perfect home for the Plains Indians?

American Indian Tribes of the West

The Desert Dwellers

The Southwest is hot and dry. The Pueblo (PWEB-low) Indians lived in the Southwest. They thought that land was holy. The Pueblos gave honor to nature. They showed honor to the spirits. They said that there were six directions. The directions were north, south, east, west, above, and below.

Each man was part of a group. The group met in a kiva. Kivas were like caves. They were dug in the ground. Women and children could not go into them.

The Pueblo homes were also called pueblos. They were made of clay or sandstone. People who lived along rivers used adobe. This river clay was used for their houses.

Pueblo Indians did not move around. They were farmers. They had fields of corn, squash, and beans. They also grew peppers and cotton. Men and boys worked the fields. The women made the meals. They wove fabric. The women also made pottery.

The Totem Pole Carvers

The Northwest is a wet area. The northwestern tribes made totem poles. They carved birds, animals, or spirits on them. The poles told about families. The best artist was picked to carve the bottom of the totem pole. That is because people can easily see the bottom.

The Indians lived in big houses. The homes were built with logs. A few families lived in each one. They were related through the mother. A special mat told people where each family lived in the home.

The tribe showed respect for food. The First Foods Ceremony (SER-uh-mo-nee) was held each spring to thank the Creator for their crops.

The men fished and hunted. They used traps, clubs, and arrows. They used harpoons to kill whales. Then, they used every part of the whale's body. The women cleaned and dried the meat and fish. They cooked the meals.

Comprehension Question

Name at least two things carved into totem poles.

American Indian Tribes of the West

The Desert Dwellers

The Pueblo (PWEB-low) Indians lived in the Southwest. They thought that land was holy. The Pueblos gave honor to nature and the spirits. They thought that there were six directions—north, south, east, west, above, and below.

Every man belonged to a religious group. The group held secret meetings in a kiva. Kivas were like caves dug in the ground. Women and children could not go into them.

The Pueblo homes were also called pueblos. They were made of clay or sandstone. People who lived along rivers used adobe. This river clay was used to make their houses.

Pueblo Indians did not move around. They were farmers. They had fields of squash, beans, and maize. Maize is another word for corn. They had smaller plots of chili peppers and cotton. Men and boys worked in the fields. The women and girls made the meals, wove fabric, and made pottery.

The Totem Pole Carvers

The northwestern tribes made totem poles. They had birds, animals, or spirits carved on them. A totem pole told the story of a family. It was good to be the "low man on the totem pole." That meant that you would carve the bottom part. The best artist was chosen to do that.

These Indians lived in large houses. They were made with red cedar logs. Several families lived in each one. The families were related through the mother. A fancy mat told visitors where each family lived inside the house.

Their ceremonies (SER-uh-mo-neez) showed respect for food and weather. The First Foods Ceremony was held each spring. In it, they thanked the Creator for their crops.

The men and boys spent time fishing and hunting. They used traps, clubs, and arrows. The women cleaned, dried, and cooked the meat and fish. The Indians used harpoons to kill whales. Then, they used every part of the whale's body.

Comprehension Question

What was carved into totem poles?

American Indian Tribes of the West

The Desert Dwellers

The Pueblo (PWEB-low) Indians lived in the Southwest. They believed that land was holy. The Pueblos gave honor to the natural and spiritual worlds. They thought there were six directions—north, south, east, west, above, and below.

Every man belonged to a religious group. The group held secret rituals in a kiva. Kivas were underground rooms. Women and children could not enter them.

The Pueblo homes were also called pueblos. They were made of clay or sandstone and other natural materials. The people who lived along rivers used river clay called adobe for their homes. Pueblos were permanent homes.

Pueblo Indians tended fields of maize, squash, and beans. They planted gardens of chili peppers, beans, and cotton. Men and boys worked in the fields. The women and girls prepared the meals, wove fabric, and made pottery.

The Totem Pole Carvers

The northwestern tribes made totem poles. The totem poles told family histories and showed people's social status through the birds, animals, or spirits carved on them. It was good to be the "low man on the totem pole." That meant that your job was to carve the lowest section. Since it was the most visible part, the best artist was chosen to carve the bottom.

These Indians lived in large, long houses made with red cedar logs. They were made to be waterproof. Several families lived in each one. The families were related through the mother. A decorated mat told visitors the location of each family's assigned living area.

They held ceremonies (SER-uh-mo-neez) to show respect for food and weather. Their First Foods Ceremony, held every spring, thanked the Creator for their crops.

The men and boys spent time fishing and hunting, using traps, clubs, and arrows. The women cleaned, dried, and cooked the meat and fish. The Indians used harpoons to kill whales. Then, they used every part of the whale's body.

Comprehension Question

Why did the northwestern tribes carve detailed totem poles?

American Indian Tribes of the West

The Desert Dwellers

The Pueblo (PWEB-low) Indians lived in the Southwest. They believed that land and the natural and spiritual worlds were sacred. The Pueblos thought there were six cardinal directions—north, south, east, west, above, and below.

Every Pueblo man belonged to a religious society that held secret rituals in a kiva, which was an underground room. Women and children could not enter the kivas.

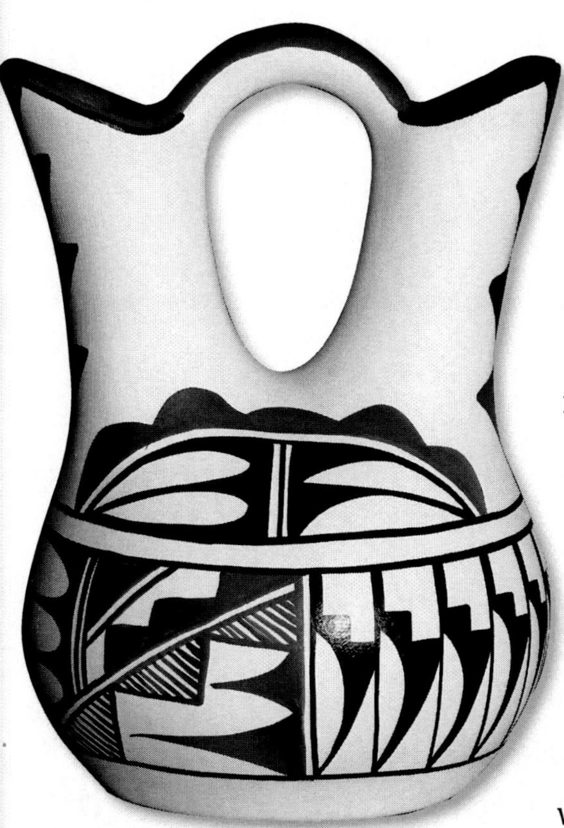

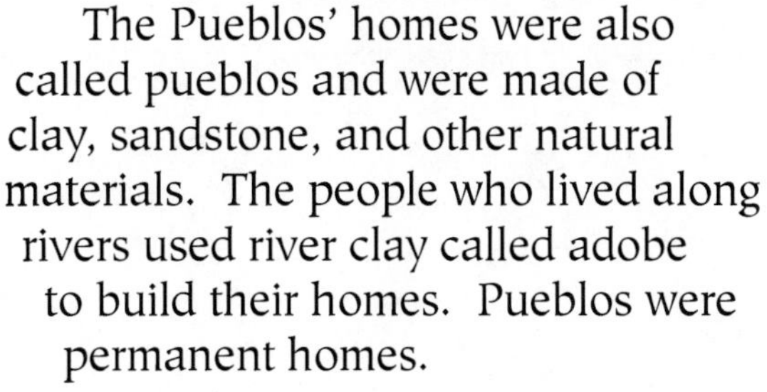

The Pueblos' homes were also called pueblos and were made of clay, sandstone, and other natural materials. The people who lived along rivers used river clay called adobe to build their homes. Pueblos were permanent homes.

Pueblo Indians tended fields of maize, squash, and beans. They planted gardens of chili peppers, beans, and cotton. Men and boys worked in the fields while the women and girls prepared the meals, wove fabric, and made pottery.

The Totem Pole Carvers

The northwestern tribes made totem poles that told family histories and showed people's social status through the birds, animals, or spirits carved on them. It was good to be the "low man on the totem pole," because it meant that your job was to carve the lowest part of the pole. Since it was the most visible part, the best artist was selected to carve the bottom.

These Indians lived in large, long houses made with red cedar logs. They were specially designed to be waterproof. Multiple families lived in each one, and a decorated mat told visitors the location of each family's assigned living area.

These tribes held ceremonies (SER-uh-mo-neez) to show respect for food and weather. Their First Foods Ceremony, held every spring, thanked the Creator for their crops.

The men and boys spent time fishing and hunting, using traps, clubs, and arrows. The women cleaned, dried, and cooked the meat and fish. When the Indians harpooned a whale, they used every part of it.

Comprehension Question

For what reasons was it important to be chosen to carve the lowest portion of the totem pole?

The New England Colonies

The North is also called New England. There were four colonies in the North. The colonies were Massachusetts, Connecticut, Rhode Island, and New Hampshire.

The Pilgrims were the first group of people to settle in the North. They came from Great Britain. The Pilgrims came over on a ship called the *Mayflower* in 1620. The second group of settlers was the Puritans. The Puritans arrived in 1629.

The Pilgrims arrived at the start of winter. It was very cold. They did not have much food. Many of them died in the cold.

The Puritans were also promised land. They had a charter. The Puritans brought a lot of food. They did well during their first winter. The Puritans came to make a new church. They wanted to make their own rules. The Puritans made lots of rules. Everyone living in the colony had to follow them.

Some people were unhappy. They did not like the rules. They left Massachusetts. They started their own colonies. This is how the rest of the New England colonies began.

Making a Living

The North was not good for farming. The ground was full of rocks. The winters were cold and lasted a long time. The colonists grew enough food to eat. But they could not grow any extra food. So, they could not make a living as farmers.

There were a lot of trees in the North. The wood from the trees was used to build ships. Some men became shipbuilders. Other men caught fish. The people ate the fish.

Many animals lived in the forests. People caught them to sell the furs. Fur traders got rich.

Comprehension Question

What kinds of jobs did men have in the North?

The New England Colonies

New England began as one large colony. Two different religious groups settled it. In the year 1620, the Pilgrims came from Great Britain. The Pilgrims landed in Plymouth Bay. The Puritans arrived in 1629. The Puritans started the Massachusetts Bay Colony.

The Pilgrims had a charter promising them land in Virginia. But their ship, the *Mayflower,* blew off course. The Pilgrims were not prepared for life in the North. They arrived just before winter. There was not enough food. Half of the colonists died that first winter.

The Puritans had a charter for land north of Plymouth. They knew how cold it would be. So, the Puritans arrived with plenty of food. They did well their first winter.

The Puritans wanted to change the Church of England. They wanted a religion that was plain and simple. They believed that all church members were equal. In the new colony, the Puritans set up their own church. It had strict rules. Everyone in Massachusetts had to follow them.

People got sick of the rules. They left Massachusetts. They began other colonies. In 1636, some people moved to the Connecticut River Valley. Roger Williams was a Puritan minister. He founded the colony of Rhode Island. By 1679, the people in New Hampshire had broken free from Massachusetts, too.

Making a Living

The North was not good for farming. The soil was too rocky. The winters were cold and long. The people grew only enough food to feed themselves. So, they had to find other ways to earn money.

There were many forests. The trees there were good for building ships. There were many animals in the forests, too. Fur traders caught them. Then they sold the fur. Some grew quite rich. Other men caught fish in the sea. This provided food for the colonists.

Comprehension Question

Life in the North was hard. What jobs did the northerners have?

The New England Colonies

New England started as one large colony. It was settled by two different religious groups. In 1620, the Pilgrims came from Great Britain on the *Mayflower*. They started a colony in Plymouth Bay. The Puritans arrived in 1629. They started the Massachusetts Bay Colony.

The Pilgrims had a charter promising them land in Virginia. But on the trip across, their ship blew off course. Unfortunately, they were unprepared for life in the North. They arrived just before winter. There was not enough food. Half of the colonists died that first winter.

The Puritans had a charter for land north of Plymouth. The Puritans arrived with food. They were prepared and did well their first winter.

The Puritans wanted to simplify the Church of England. They did not believe in fancy ceremonies. The Puritans thought that all church members should be equal. They set up their own church in the new colony. The church made strict rules that everyone in Massachusetts had to follow. This was true even if the people were not Puritans.

Over time, people left Massachusetts. They started other colonies. In 1636, small groups of people moved to the Connecticut River Valley. Roger Williams, a Puritan minister, founded the colony of Rhode Island. By 1679, the colonists in New Hampshire had broken away from Massachusetts, too.

Making a Living

The northerners quickly learned that their new home was not very good for farming. The soil was rocky. The winters were cold and long. The colonists could only grow enough food to feed their own families. They had to find other ways to earn money.

In the early years, most colonists lived in towns along the ocean. There the men became shipbuilders, traders, and fishermen. The inland forests provided wood for building ships. They also were home to a variety of fur-bearing animals. This helped fur traders grow rich. Fishermen in the port towns provided food for the colonists of the region.

Comprehension Question

How did geography affect life in the northern colonies?

The New England Colonies

New England started as one large colony settled by two different religious groups. In 1620, the Pilgrims came from Great Britain on the *Mayflower* and started a colony in Plymouth Bay. The Puritans arrived in 1629 and started the Massachusetts Bay Colony.

The Pilgrims had a charter promising them land in Virginia, but on the trip across, their ship blew off course. Unfortunately, they were unprepared for life in the North. They arrived just before winter, and there was not enough food. Half of the colonists died that first winter.

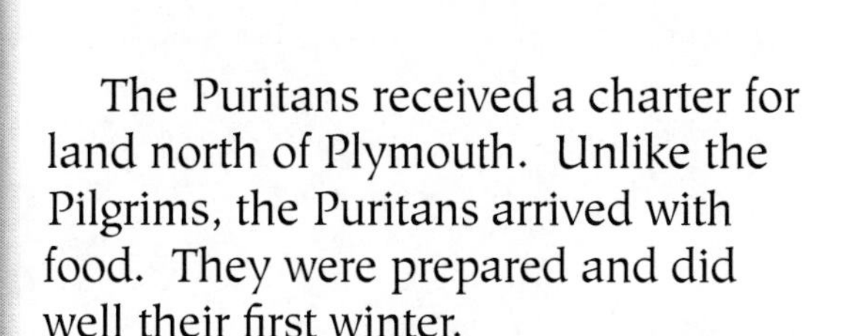

The Puritans received a charter for land north of Plymouth. Unlike the Pilgrims, the Puritans arrived with food. They were prepared and did well their first winter.

The Puritans wanted to simplify the Church of England. They did not believe that religion should have fancy ceremonies. Puritans thought that all church members should be equal. The Puritans set up their own church in the new colony and made strict rules that everyone in Massachusetts had to follow, even if they were not Puritans.

Over time, people left Massachusetts to start other colonies. In 1636, small groups of people moved to the Connecticut River Valley. Roger Williams, a Puritan minister, founded the colony of Rhode Island. By 1679, the colonists in New Hampshire had broken away from Massachusetts to form a new colony.

Making a Living

The northerners quickly learned that their new home was not very good for farming because the soil was rocky, and the winters were cold and long. The colonists could only grow enough food to feed their own families. The people living in New England had to find other ways to earn money.

In the early years, most colonists lived in towns along the ocean, and the men became shipbuilders, traders, and fishermen. The inland forests provided both wood for building ships and a variety of fur-bearing animals, which helped fur traders grow rich. Fishermen in the port towns provided food for the colonists of the region.

Comprehension Question

In what ways was life in the North difficult? How did the northerners cope?

The Middle Colonies

Settling the Middle Colonies

The Dutch and Swedish started the first middle colony. The Dutch named it New Netherland (NETH-uhr-land). King Charles II was the king of Great Britain. He wanted New Netherland. He said that he would take it by force. But the people did not want to fight. They gave up the land in the year 1664. The king gave it to his brother James. James split it into two colonies. They were New York and New Jersey.

William Penn started Pennsylvania and Delaware. They were the other two middle colonies.

William Penn's Woods

William Penn was a Quaker. The Quakers were a group of people. They said that all people were equal. They did not believe in war. The people in Great Britain did not like them. So, Mr. Penn wanted to go away.

William Penn's father had lent money to King Charles II. Penn went to the king. Penn said that he did not want the money. He wanted land in the New World. So the king gave land to Penn in 1681. There were many trees on the land. People called it Penn's Woods. It is now called Pennsylvania.

William Penn let the people be free. They did not have to belong to a church. Any man could vote or hold office. Pennsylvania was the center of colonial America. In the late 1700s, important things happened there. Its capital city was Philadelphia.

Bread Basket Colonies

The people cleared the land for farms in the middle colonies. They grew grain. Grain is used to make bread. So, people called them the "bread basket" colonies. The farmers sold grain and cows to the other colonies. The people in the middle colonies also made iron. They used it for guns and tools.

Many rivers flowed through the middle colonies. This made trading easy. Farmers put their crops on boats. The boats sailed to big ports. The biggest ports were in New York City and Philadelphia. There, the crops were loaded onto large ships.

Comprehension Question

Name at least two ways that the middle colonies were important to colonial America.

The Middle Colonies

Settling the Middle Colonies

The Dutch and Swedish settled the first middle colony. The Dutch named the colony New Netherland (NETH-uhr-land). King Charles II of England wanted New Netherland. In the year 1664, he said that he would take the land by force. But the settlers gave up without a fight. Then the king gave the land to his brother James. James split the land into New York and New Jersey.

William Penn owned Pennsylvania and Delaware. They were the other two middle colonies.

William Penn's Woods

William Penn belonged to a group known as the Quakers. They said that all people were equal. They did not believe in fighting. The people in Great Britain did not like the Quakers. So Penn wanted to leave.

King Charles II had once borrowed money from William Penn's father. Penn asked the king to repay him with land in the New World. In 1681, the king gave Penn land. People called it Penn's Woods. Today it is called Pennsylvania. Penn let the people there have freedom. They did not have to belong to a church. Men of any religion could vote or hold office.

This colony became the center of colonial America. During the late 1700s, important things happened there. Its capital city was Philadelphia.

Bread Basket Colonies

The middle colonies had hills and rich soil. The colonists cleared the land for farms. They grew a lot of grain. Grain is used to make bread. So, people called them the "bread basket" colonies. The farmers sent wheat, barley, oats, and cows to the southern colonies and to the British West Indies. These colonies also made iron. Iron was used for guns and tools.

Many rivers flowed through this area. They made trading easy. Farmers who lived inland sent their goods on boats. The boats sailed to the big port cities in New York and Pennsylvania. There, things could be loaded onto sea-going ships.

Comprehension Question

In what ways were the middle colonies important to colonial America?

The Middle Colonies

Settling the Middle Colonies

The Dutch and Swedish settled the first middle colony. The Dutch named its colony New Netherland (NETH-uhr-land). New York City was called New Amsterdam.

In 1664, King Charles II of England wanted to take over New Netherland. He threatened to start a war. The Dutch and Swedish settlers gave up the land without a fight. Then the king gave the land to his brother James, the Duke of York. James split the land into New York and New Jersey.

William Penn started the other middle colonies, Delaware and Pennsylvania.

William Penn's Woods

William Penn belonged to the Society of Friends. This was a religious group known as the Quakers. Quakers thought that all people were equal. They did not believe in fighting. The Quakers were disliked in Great Britain, so Penn wanted to leave.

King Charles II had once borrowed money from William Penn's father. Penn asked the king to repay that debt with land in the New World. In 1681, the king gave him Penn's Woods. This is now called Pennsylvania. Penn made sure that in Pennsylvania, people had religious freedom. This meant that they did not have to belong to a specific church. Members of any religion could vote or be elected to office.

Pennsylvania grew to be the center of colonial America. The capital of the colonies was in Philadelphia. During the late 1700s, many important events occurred in this city.

Bread Basket Colonies

The middle colonies had hills and rich soil. So, the people cleared the land for farms. People called these colonies the "bread basket" colonies because grain was so plentiful. The farmers exported wheat, barley, oats, and cows to the southern colonies and the British West Indies. These colonies also made iron, which was used to make guns and tools.

Many rivers flowed through the area. They made trading easy for farmers who lived inland. These farmers sent their goods on boats to the big port cities of Philadelphia and New York. There, things were loaded onto sea-going ships.

Comprehension Question

How did farming in the middle colonies affect the success of colonial America?

The Middle Colonies

Establishing the Middle Colonies

The Dutch and Swedish settled the first middle colony. The Dutch colonists named the colony New Netherland (NETH-uhr-land). New York City was called New Amsterdam.

King Charles II of England announced that he wanted to own New Netherland in 1664. He threatened to send soldiers to take it by force. The Dutch and Swedish colonists did not want to fight. They simply gave up the land. The king gave the land to his brother James, the Duke of York. James divided it into New York and New Jersey.

Later William Penn founded the two other middle colonies, Pennsylvania and Delaware.

William Penn's Woods

William Penn belonged to the Society of Friends, a religious group known as the Quakers. Quakers thought that all people were equal, and they did not believe in fighting. However, the Quakers were disliked in Great Britain, and Penn wanted to leave the country.

Years before, King Charles II had borrowed money from Penn's father. So, Penn asked the king to repay that debt with land in the New World. In 1681, the king granted him Penn's Woods, which is the area now called Pennsylvania. Penn made sure that people had religious freedom in his colony. Members of any religion could vote or be elected to office.

Pennsylvania became the center of colonial America. During the late 1700s, many important historical events occurred in Philadelphia, its capital city.

Bread Basket Colonies

The middle colonies manufactured iron, which was made into guns, axes, and tools. There were hills with fertile soil, so the people cleared the land for farms. Farmers grew and exported wheat, barley, oats, and livestock to the southern colonies and the British West Indies. Grain was so abundant that people referred to these colonies as the "bread basket" colonies.

Many rivers flowed through this region, which made trading easy for farmers living inland. They shipped goods on boats to the ports of Philadelphia and New York City, where their products were loaded onto sea-going ships.

Comprehension Question

In what ways did the middle colonies affect the success of the northern and southern colonies?

The Southern Colonies

About 100 men and boys sailed to Virginia in 1607. They set up a settlement. They named their new home Jamestown. They did not plant crops. They looked for gold. Just a few of the men built good homes. So, most of them died the first year. Then John Smith took charge. He made a new rule. If a man did not work, he did not eat. The people began to work.

The South had four more colonies. In 1634, Lord Baltimore started Maryland. He was a Catholic who had been treated badly in Great Britain. He wanted Catholics to have a safe place to live.

In 1663, North and South Carolina were settled as one colony. They stayed one colony until the 1700s.

Georgia was the last colony settled. In 1732, James Oglethorpe (OH-guhl-thorp) went there. He built forts. This was to keep the English colonies safe from the Spanish. The Spanish lived in Florida. It is just south of Georgia.

Cash Crops and Plantations

The South had good soil. Men had big farms called plantations (plan-TAY-shuhns). They grew crops to get cash. They sold these crops to Great Britain. Virginia made a lot of money selling tobacco. The Carolinas grew tobacco and corn. Maryland did, too. South Carolina and Georgia planted rice. By the 1740s, South Carolina grew indigo. This plant is used to make a dark blue dye.

It was hard work to plant and take care of the crops. At first the farm owners had indentured servants (in-DEN-shured SIR-vuhntz). These men and women worked for years. They did this to pay for the cost of their trip to the New World. By the late 1600s, the farm owners had slaves. Most of the slaves came from Africa.

Early Southern Governments

The House of Burgesses (BURR-juhs-uhs) met in 1619. It was Virginia's first government. The men who owned land picked its members. Maryland had a government like this, too.

James Oglethorpe ruled Georgia for 20 years. He made every decision. Then, the British king said he wanted to control Georgia. After that, the king named the leaders.

Comprehension Question

What was the rule that John Smith made in Virginia?

The Southern Colonies

About 100 men and boys sailed to Virginia in the year 1607. They named their new settlement Jamestown. The men should have planted crops and built homes. Instead they spent their time looking for gold. Within a year, most of them had died of sickness or hunger. Then Captain John Smith took charge. Under his rule, those who did not work were left to starve. Slowly the colony grew successful.

The South had four other colonies. In 1634, Lord Baltimore founded Maryland. As a Catholic, he had been mistreated for his ideas. He wanted religious freedom. He kept this in mind as he set up Maryland.

North and South Carolina started as one colony in 1663. They stayed that way until the 1700s.

Georgia was the last colony settled. In 1732, James Oglethorpe (OH-guhl-thorp) went there and built forts. He did this to keep the English safe from the Spanish. The Spanish lived in Florida.

Cash Crops and Plantations

The land in the South was rich. The growing season was long. Rivers kept the soil moist. Big plantations (plan-TAY-shuhns) grew cash crops to sell to Great Britain. Virginia's main cash crop was tobacco. North Carolina, South Carolina, and Maryland raised corn and tobacco. South Carolina and Georgia planted rice. By the 1740s, South Carolina grew indigo. This plant is used to make a dark blue dye.

It was hard work to plant and tend crops. At first the owners had indentured servants (in-DEN-shured SIR-vuhntz). These men and women paid for their trips to the New World by working on the farms. But by the late 1600s, the plantation owners had slaves from Africa.

Early Southern Governments

In 1619, the House of Burgesses (BURR-juhs-uhs) became the ruling body of Virginia. The members of the government were chosen by the male landowners. Maryland had a similar elected assembly.

In Georgia, James Oglethorpe controlled the colonists for 20 years. He made every decision. Then the British king made the land a royal colony. After that, the king picked the leaders and council members.

Comprehension Question

Why was John Smith's rule important?

The Southern Colonies

The Virginia Company of London founded the first southern colony. In 1607, it sent about 100 men and boys to Virginia. They named their new home Jamestown after King James.

The men looked for gold instead of planting crops or building homes. And, the area they chose was swampy. Mosquitoes spread disease. By 1608, most of the men had died. Then, John Smith took charge. Under his rule, those who did not work were left to starve. Slowly the colony grew successful.

There were four other colonies in the South. In 1634, Lord Baltimore founded Maryland for religious freedom. As a Catholic, he had been mistreated in Great Britain.

North and South Carolina started as one large colony in 1663. They remained that way until the early 1700s.

Georgia was the last colony settled. In 1732, King George II granted the land to James Oglethorpe (OH-guhl-thorp). He settled it and built forts. This kept the English safe from the Spanish in Florida.

Cash Crops and Plantations

The land in the South was fertile, and the growing season long. Rivers kept the soil moist. Cash crops were grown on large plantations (plan-TAY-shuhns). Virginia's main cash crop was tobacco. The Carolinas and Maryland grew corn and tobacco. Rice proved profitable (PROF-it-uh-buhl) for South Carolina and Georgia. By the 1740s, South Carolina grew indigo. This plant is used to make a dark blue dye.

Planting and tending crops took lots of work. At first the planters used indentured servants. These men and women paid for the cost of their trip to the New World by working on the farms. But by the late 1600s, the plantation owners were using slaves from Africa.

Early Southern Governments

In 1619, the House of Burgesses (BURR-juhs-uhs) became the ruling body of Virginia. The members of the government were chosen by the male landowners. Maryland had a similar elected assembly.

In Georgia, Oglethorpe controlled the colonists for 20 years. He made every decision. Then, the British king made the land a royal colony. From then on, the king picked the leaders and council members.

Comprehension Question

Why did John Smith have to make rules for the men living in Virginia?

The Southern Colonies

The Virginia Company of London founded the first southern colony when it sent about 100 men and boys to Virginia in 1607. The men named their settlement Jamestown in honor of King James. At first, they searched for gold instead of planting crops or building homes. The area they settled was swampy, and within a year most of the men had died from hunger and diseases spread by mosquitoes. Finally, Captain John Smith took over leadership, and under his rule those who did not work were left to starve. Gradually, the colony grew successful.

Four other colonies made up the South. In 1634, Lord Baltimore founded Maryland for religious freedom because in Great Britain he was mistreated as a Catholic. North and South Carolina started as a single colony in 1663 and stayed that way until the early 1700s.

In 1732, King George II granted James Oglethorpe (OH-guhl-thorp) the land for the colony of Georgia. Oglethorpe settled it and built forts to protect the English from the Spaniards in Florida.

Cash Crops and Plantations

The South's land was rich and its growing season long. Rivers kept the soil moist. Cash crops grew on large plantations (plan-TAY-shuhns). Virginia's main cash crop was tobacco. The Carolinas and Maryland raised corn and tobacco. Rice proved profitable (PROF-it-uh-buhl) for South Carolina and Georgia. By the 1740s, South Carolina grew indigo, a plant used to make a dark blue dye.

Planting, tending, and harvesting crops took many laborers. The plantation owners started out using indentured servants. These men and women paid for their passage to the New World by working on the plantations for years. But by the late 1600s, plantation owners started purchasing African slaves instead of using indentured servants.

Early Southern Governments

In 1619, male landowners in Virginia elected the members of the House of Burgesses (BURR-juhs-uhs). This was the first elected representative government in North America. Maryland had a similar assembly.

James Oglethorpe controlled the colonists in Georgia for 20 years. He made every decision until the British king made the land a royal colony. From that point on, the king named the leaders and council members.

Comprehension Question

In what ways did John Smith's rule affect life in Virginia?

Slavery in the New World

A plantation (plan-TAY-shuhn) is a huge farm. It was hard work to run a plantation. The colonists grew tobacco and cotton. They needed help. So, they put Africans to work in their fields. In 1619, a ship came to Jamestown. It held 60 Africans. They had been baptized on the ship. So, they were Christians. That meant they could not be slaves. They were indentured servants (in-DEN-shured SIR-vuhntz). This meant that they had to work on a farm. This is how they paid for the trip. After seven years, they were set free.

After that, the slave trade began. Slave traders went to Africa. There, they picked up people. Men, women, and children were taken from their homes. They did not want to come. They were forced. The Africans were put onto ships. Then, they were taken to the colonies. But they were not baptized. So, they were thought of as less than human.

The slave traders wanted to make lots of money. They put too many people on the ships. The slave traders did not give the Africans enough food or water. The trip across the ocean was the Middle Passage. Many Africans died on the trip.

From Africa to America

At last, the ship reached the shore. Then, the people were sold. Men who owned land would offer money to buy the Africans. The one who offered the most got the slave. The slaves were bought one by one. Families were split up. One man might buy a mother. Another might buy a child. They might never see each other again.

The slaves led hard lives. They had no rights. They were thought of as things. Their owners could do anything to them. Slaves could be sold. Each day slave families did not know if they would be together.

Many Africans did important things in early America. Phillis Wheatley wrote poetry about her life. And, Benjamin Banneker helped design Washington, D.C.

By the year 1860, there were four million slaves in the United States. Just a few of them were set free. It took almost 200 years and a war to end slavery in America.

Comprehension Question

Name at least two things slaves did in the colonies.

Slavery in the New World

A plantation (plan-TAY-shuhn) is a huge farm. It was hard work running a plantation. The colonists needed help. They chose to get Africans to work in their tobacco and cotton fields. In the fall of 1619, a ship came to Jamestown. The governor traded food for 60 Africans. These people had been baptized during the trip. Now they were Christians. So, they could not be slaves. They were indentured servants (in-DEN-shured SIR-vuhntz) instead. They had to work on a farm for seven years. At the end of that time they were free.

Soon after, the slave trade started. Slave traders grew rich by sending ships to Africa. There, they picked up human cargo. These men, women, and children had been taken from their homes. They were put onto ships and taken to the colonies. The Africans were not baptized. As a result, they were thought of as sub-human.

The trip across the ocean on these ships was called the Middle Passage. The slave traders only wanted to make money. They put too many people onto their ships. The slave traders did not give the Africans enough food or water. Many Africans died during the awful trip.

From Africa to the Plantation

At last the ships reached the colonies. Then, the traders sold their captives. They held auctions (AUK-shuhnz). Landowners would bid on the people. The one who bid the most money got the slave. The slaves were bought one at a time. Families could be split up. Different people could buy parents and children! They might never see each other again.

The slaves had tough lives with no rights and no choices. Slaves were thought of as things, just like a book or a tool. The owners could do anything they wanted to them. The slaves could be sold at any time. Slave families never knew if they would stay together.

There were many Africans who contributed to early America. Phillis Wheatley wrote beautiful poetry. And, Benjamin Banneker contributed to the design and layout of Washington, D.C.

By the year 1860, there were four million slaves in the United States. Few were given their freedom. It took almost 200 years and a war to end slavery in America.

Comprehension Question

How did the slaves change life in the colonies?

Slavery in the New World

It was hard work settling new land. The colonists decided to use Africans to work on their tobacco and cotton plantations (plan-TAY-shuhns). A plantation is a huge farm with many fields. In the fall of 1619, Jamestown governor George Yeardley traded food for 60 Africans. He bought them to work on the plantations. Since these people had been baptized during the voyage, they were considered Christians. This meant that they could not be slaves. Instead, they were indentured servants (in-DEN-shured SIR-vuhntz). They had to work on a plantation for seven years. At the end of that time they were free.

Soon after, the Trans-Atlantic Slave Trade started. Slave traders grew wealthy by sending British and colonial ships to Africa and picking up human captives. These men, women, and children were kidnapped from their homes. They were loaded onto ships and taken to the colonies. They were not baptized, and so they were considered sub-human.

The trip across the ocean on the slave ships was called the Middle Passage. The slave traders were greedy. They wanted to make as much money as possible. They packed far too many people onto their ships. The slave traders did not give the Africans enough food or water. Many Africans died during the awful journey.

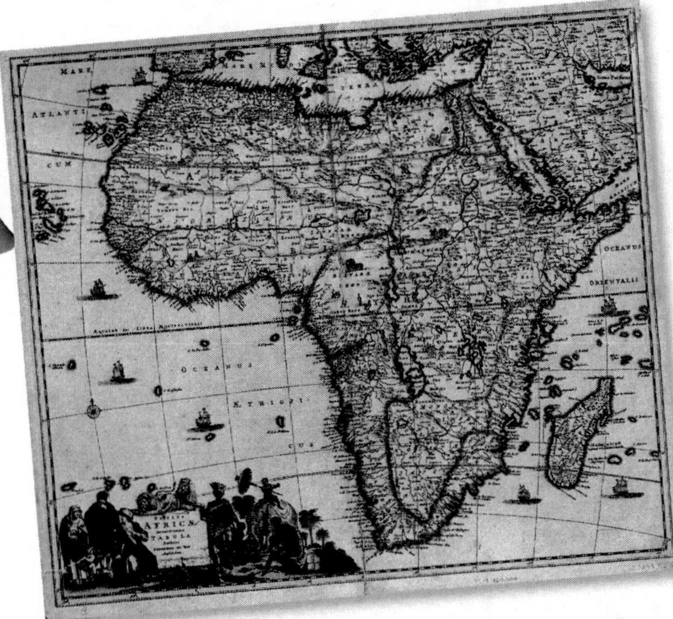

From Africa to the Plantation

After the ships reached the colonies, the traders sold their captives. The slaves were usually sold at auctions (AUK-shuhnz). Landowners bid on the captives. Whoever bid the most money owned the new slave. Each slave was bid on separately. This meant that families were often split up. Different people could purchase husbands and wives, parents and children! They might never see each other again.

The slaves had tough lives with no rights and no choices. Slaves were thought of as property, just like pieces of furniture. The owners could do whatever they wanted to them. They could sell the slaves at any time. Slave families never knew how long they would be together.

Africans made important contributions to early America. Phillis Wheatley wrote beautiful poetry about life in the North. Benjamin Banneker contributed to the design and layout of Washington, D.C.

By 1860, there were four million slaves in the United States. Few were granted freedom, and even fewer bought their freedom. It took almost 200 years and a war to rid America of slavery.

Comprehension Question

In what ways did the Africans affect life in the New World?

Slavery in the New World

It was hard work settling new land, so the colonists decided to use Africans to work on their tobacco and cotton plantations (plan-TAY-shuhns). In the fall of 1619, Jamestown governor George Yeardley traded a ship full of food for 60 Africans. He purchased them to work on the tobacco plantations. Since these people had been baptized during the voyage, they were considered Christians, and this meant that they could not be slaves. Instead, they were indentured servants (in-DEN-shured SIR-vuhntz) and had to work on a plantation for about seven years to earn their freedom.

Soon after, the Trans-Atlantic Slave Trade started. Slave traders grew wealthy by sending British and colonial ships to Africa and picking up human captives. These men, women, and children, who had been kidnapped from their homes, were loaded onto ships and taken to the colonies. They were not baptized and were therefore considered sub-human.

The trip across the ocean on the slave ships was called the Middle Passage. The slave traders were greedy and wanted to make as much money as possible. They packed far too many people onto their ships and did not provide them with enough food or water. Many Africans died during the horrific journey.

From Africa to the Plantation

After the ships reached the colonies, the traders sold their captives, most frequently at auctions (AUK-shuhnz). Landowners bid on the captives. Whoever bid the most money owned the new slave. Each individual was bid on separately, and this meant that families were often split up. Different people could purchase husbands and wives, parents and children! They might never see each other again.

The slaves had difficult lives with no rights and no choices. Slaves were considered property, just like pieces of furniture. The owners could do whatever they wanted to them and could sell them at any time. Slave families never knew how long they would stay together.

Even with these challenges, Africans made important contributions to early America. Phillis Wheatley wrote beautiful poetry about life in the North. Benjamin Banneker contributed to the design and layout of Washington, D.C.

By 1860, there were four million slaves in the United States. Few were granted freedom, and even fewer bought their freedom. It took almost 200 years and a war to rid America of slavery.

Comprehension Question

In what ways did the Africans positively affect change in the colonies?

Causes of the American Revolution

Nobody Likes Taxes

Great Britain needed money. It passed the Stamp Act. This meant that any paper with writing on it must have a stamp. Each stamp cost a few cents. A stamp was needed on each newspaper. Even playing cards had to have a stamp. This made the colonists mad. They would not pay. Mobs yelled at the men who came to sell the stamps.

The British were shocked. They saw that the tax would not work. So it was repealed. Repealed means it was stopped. Yet, Great Britain still needed money. So, it passed the Townshend (TOWNS-end) Acts. These acts taxed glass, paint, paper, lead, and tea. No one in Great Britain had to pay these taxes. The colonists did not want to pay. People gave speeches to protest. People in the colonies stopped buying British goods.

Things Go Too Far

Then, Great Britain sent 4,000 troops to Boston. On March 5, 1770, a colonist got into a fight with a British soldier. More people came. The colonists threw rocks and ice. Soon, eight more soldiers came. Someone yelled, "Fire!" The troops shot into the crowd. Five people died. The people called this the Boston Massacre. A *massacre* is when many people die.

Next came the Tea Act. Great Britain let just a few shops in the colonies sell tea. Samuel Adams gave a speech. He told people to fight back. In December 1773, some men dressed like Indians. These men went onto British ships at night. They opened 342 boxes of tea. They threw the tea into the water. The people called this the "Boston Tea Party."

The Boston Tea Party made King George III mad. He made strong new laws. The people called them the Intolerable (in-TOL-uhr-uh-buhl) Acts. The word *intolerable* means too hard to live with. One of these acts shut down Boston Harbor. No one could fish. This put half of the men in that town out of work. Another law let British troops live in people's homes!

Most colonists did not want to fight. But, the king had made a mistake. These laws made the colonists really dislike the king. They wanted to be free.

Comprehension Question

Describe at least two of the British acts.

Causes of the American Revolution

Nobody Likes Taxes

Great Britain needed money. Its government passed the Stamp Act. This act required stamps on all printed paper. A stamp was needed on each newspaper. One was needed on playing cards. Even a wedding license needed a stamp. This made the colonists mad. They would not pay. Angry mobs scared the men who came to sell the stamps. By the time the tax was supposed to start, no one was left to get the money!

The British were shocked. They saw that the tax would not work. So it was repealed. To repeal a tax means to cancel it. Yet, the nation still needed money. So, the government passed the Townshend (TOWNS-end) Acts. These acts taxed glass, paint, paper, lead, and tea. No one in Great Britain had to pay these taxes. The colonists did not want to, either. People gave speeches. They wrote articles. They convinced the colonists to stop buying British goods.

Things Go Too Far

Then, the British leaders sent 4,000 troops to Boston. On March 5, 1770, a colonist got into a fight with a British guard. More people joined in. They threw rocks and ice. Soon, eight more soldiers came. Someone yelled, "Fire!" The troops shot into the crowd. Five colonists died. The Americans called this the Boston Massacre. A massacre is the killing of many people.

Next came the Tea Act. It let just a few shop owners sell tea. The colonists hated Britain's control over them. Samuel Adams gave speeches. He told people to fight back against the Tea Act. One night in December 1773, some men dressed as Indians. They sneaked aboard British ships. They broke open 342 chests of tea. They threw the tea into Boston Harbor. The people called this the "Boston Tea Party."

After that, King George III was mad. He made harsh new laws. The colonists called them the Intolerable (in-TOL-uhr-uh-buhl) Acts. One law closed Boston Harbor. No one could fish in the sea. No one could use the ocean for trade. This put half of the men in Boston out of work. Another law made colonists let British soldiers live in their homes!

The king had made a big mistake. Before this, most colonists had not wanted to fight. Now, these laws made them dislike the king. More people longed to be free.

Comprehension Question

Describe the three British acts included in this text.

Causes of the American Revolution

Nobody Likes Taxes

Great Britain needed money. Parliament (PAR-luh-muhnt) passed the Stamp Act. It required stamps on any printed paper, including newspapers and marriage licenses. The stamps cost money. This made the colonists mad, and they refused to pay. Angry mobs scared the men who came to sell the stamps. By the time the tax was supposed to start, no one was left to collect the money!

The British were shocked. They saw that the tax would not work. So Parliament repealed it. Yet, the nation still needed money. So, the government passed the Townshend (TOWNS-end) Acts. This taxed glass, paint, paper, lead, and tea. No one in Great Britain had to pay these taxes. The colonists did not want to, either. People gave speeches and wrote articles. They convinced the colonists to stop buying British goods.

Things Go Too Far

Then, the British leaders sent 4,000 soldiers to Boston. On March 5, 1770, a colonist got into an argument with a British guard. More people joined in. Colonists threw rocks and ice. Soon, eight more soldiers came. When someone yelled, "Fire!" the soldiers shot into the crowd. They killed five colonists. The Americans called this the Boston Massacre.

Next, Parliament passed the Tea Act. This act allowed just a few shop owners to sell tea. The colonists hated Britain's control over their economy. Samuel Adams gave speeches and told people to fight back against the Tea Act. One night in December 1773, men dressed as Indians and sneaked aboard British ships. They broke open 342 chests of tea and threw the tea into Boston Harbor. The people cheered for this "Boston Tea Party."

After that, King George III cracked down. He made harsh new laws that the colonists called the Intolerable (in-TOL-uhr-uh-buhl) Acts. One law closed Boston Harbor. This meant that no one could fish or use the ocean for trade. It put half of the men in Boston out of work. Another forced colonists to let British soldiers live in their homes!

The king had made a big mistake. Many colonists had never before seen a reason to fight. Now, these laws were so hated that more people longed for freedom.

Comprehension Question

Why did the colonists in Boston think the British acts were unfair?

Causes of the American Revolution

Nobody Likes Taxes

Great Britain needed money, so Parliament (PAR-luh-muhnt) passed the Stamp Act. This act required stamps on any printed paper, including newspapers and marriage licenses. The stamps cost money. This infuriated the colonists, and they refused to pay. Angry mobs frightened the men who came to sell the stamps. By the time the tax was to officially start, nobody was left to collect the money!

The British were shocked. They realized that the tax would not work, and Parliament repealed it. However, the nation still needed money, so the government passed the Townshend (TOWNS-end) Acts to tax glass, paint, paper, lead, and tea. Nobody in Great Britain had to pay these taxes, and the colonists did not want to, either. People gave speeches and wrote articles convincing the colonists to boycott British goods. The colonists refused to purchase anything from Great Britain.

Things Go Too Far

The boycott frustrated the British leaders. They sent 4,000 soldiers to Boston. On March 5, 1770, a colonist got into an argument with a British guard. More people joined in. Colonists threw rocks and ice. Soon, eight more soldiers came. When somebody yelled, "Fire!" the soldiers shot into the crowd, killing five colonists. The Americans called this the Boston Massacre.

Then, Parliament passed the Tea Act, which allowed just a few shop owners to sell tea. The colonists disliked that Britain had control over their economy. Samuel Adams gave speeches and told people to defy the Tea Act. One night in December 1773, men dressed as Indians sneaked aboard British ships, broke open 342 chests of tea, and threw the tea into Boston Harbor. The people cheered for this "Boston Tea Party."

After that, King George III cracked down with harsh new laws that made the colonists furious. They called them the Intolerable (in-TOL-uhr-uh-buhl) Acts. One law closed Boston Harbor, which meant that nobody could fish or use the ocean for trade. This put half of the men in Boston out of work. Another law forced colonists to allow British soldiers to live in their homes!

The king had made a huge mistake. Many colonists had never before seen a reason to fight, but these laws were so disliked that now these people longed for freedom.

Comprehension Question

Use details to explain why the British acts upset the colonists living in Boston.

The Declaration of Independence

In June 1776, a group of men met. They had to make choices for the colonists. This group was called the Second Continental (kon-tuh-NEN-tuhl) Congress. One man had an idea. He wanted the colonies to be free of British rule. The congress decided to write a paper telling why the people wanted to be free.

An Important Task

Five men were picked to write the paper. Four of the men were from the North. Their names were John Adams, Benjamin Franklin, Robert Livingston, and Roger Sherman. The one man from the South was Thomas Jefferson.

The men talked about their job. They thought that it would be too hard to write the paper as a group. Just one person should write. Jefferson was a good writer. The men chose him.

The members of this group told Thomas Jefferson what he must say. He had to say what makes a good government. He had to say how unfair the king was. And, he had to say that the colonists were free. They were no longer under Great Britain's rule.

An Important Vote

Thomas Jefferson wrote and wrote. He worked day and night. When he was done, he showed the paper to the group. The men liked what he had done.

Next, the group showed the draft of the Declaration of Independence to the congress. Most of the men thought it was good.

Congress talked about declaring independence from Britain. In fact, they spent the next few days talking about it. They thought about what Patrick Henry had once said. He said, "Give me liberty or give me death!" Liberty means freedom.

On July 2, the men voted to declare independence. They knew that it would be hard. They knew that men would die. But they wanted to be free. Then they could have a new government. It would be the first of its kind on Earth. There would be no king. The people would run things. They would make their own choices.

Comprehension Question

Name the three things Thomas Jefferson had to state in the paper.

The Declaration of Independence

In June 1776, the Second Continental (kon-tuh-NEN-tuhl) Congress met. This group of men met to make choices for the colonists. One of them had an idea. He wanted Congress to say that the colonies were independent. The Congress decided to prepare an essay. It would tell why the colonists wanted to be free of British rule.

An Important Task

The congress chose a group of five men. Four of them were from the North. Their names were John Adams, Benjamin Franklin, Robert Livingston, and Roger Sherman. The only man from the South was Thomas Jefferson.

The five men met. They talked about their task. They thought that it would be too hard to write the essay as a group. Just one person should write it. Thomas Jefferson was a gifted writer. So, the men chose him to be the writer.

The group members told Jefferson the things he must include. First, he had to tell what makes a good government. Then, he had to tell why King George III was an unjust ruler. And, he had to state that the colonists were free of Great Britain's rule.

An Important Vote

When Thomas Jefferson finished, he showed the group what he had done. They were pleased. They thought that he had done a good job.

Then, the group showed Jefferson's draft of the Declaration of Independence to Congress. Most of the men liked it. They knew they had to decide whether or not to declare independence. They spent the next few days talking about it. They thought about the words that Patrick Henry had once said. He stated, "Give me liberty or give me death!" Liberty means freedom.

On July 2, the idea to declare independence passed. Thomas Jefferson's words had inspired the others. They knew that it would be hard. They knew that men would die. But they wanted freedom. Then they could make a government unlike any ever seen on Earth. Common people, not the king, would run the government.

Comprehension Question

What three key ideas did the men want Thomas Jefferson to state in this essay?

The Declaration of Independence

In June 1776, a delegate to the Second Continental (kon-tuh-NEN-tuhl) Congress made a proposal. He wanted Congress to declare the colonies independent from Great Britain. Congress decided to prepare a document. It would describe the reasons the colonists wanted to be free of British rule.

An Important Task

The congress chose a group of five men. Four of them were northerners: John Adams, Benjamin Franklin, Robert Livingston, and Roger Sherman. The only southerner was Thomas Jefferson, a quiet man from Virginia.

The five men met to discuss how to continue. They decided it would be too hard to write the document as a group. It would be better to have a single person compose it. Jefferson had prepared some important papers in the past. The men knew that he was a gifted writer. So, they chose him to write the document.

The committee members told Jefferson the three things he must include. First, he had to describe what makes a good government. Then, he had to explain why King George III was an unfair ruler. Finally, he had to state that the colonists were declaring themselves free of Great Britain's rule.

An Important Vote

When Jefferson finished, he showed what he had done to the group. They were pleased with his work. They thought that he had done a good job explaining the important ideas.

On June 28, the group presented Jefferson's rough draft of the Declaration of Independence to Congress. Most of the delegates liked it. They decided to make a choice about whether or not to declare independence. They spent the next few days in debate. They recalled the words that Patrick Henry had said the year before in a speech. He had stated, "Give me liberty or give me death!"

Finally, on July 2, the proposal to declare independence passed. Jefferson's words had inspired the other men. They knew it would be difficult. They knew it would require bloodshed. But they wanted freedom. Then they could create a government unlike any ever seen on Earth.

Comprehension Question

In your own words, explain what Thomas Jefferson had to say in this document.

The Declaration of Independence

In June 1776, a delegate to the Second Continental (kon-tuh-NEN-tuhl) Congress proposed that Congress declare the colonies' independence from Great Britain. Congress decided to prepare a document. It would detail the reasons the colonists wanted to be free of British rule. Having this document ready would save time when the big decision was made.

An Important Task

The congress chose a committee of five men. Four of them were northerners: John Adams, Benjamin Franklin, Robert Livingston, and Roger Sherman. The only southerner was Thomas Jefferson, a quiet delegate from Virginia.

The committee met to discuss how to proceed. They decided it would be too hard to write the document as a group and that it would be better to have a single person compose it. Jefferson had prepared some important papers in the past, and the committee knew he was a gifted writer. Thus, they selected him to write the document.

The committee members told Jefferson the three things he must include. First, he had to describe what makes a good government. Then, he had to explain why King George III was not a fair ruler. Finally, he had to announce that the colonists were declaring themselves free of Great Britain's rule.

An Important Vote

When Jefferson finished, he showed what he had written to the committee. They were pleased with his work, and they felt he had done a good job explaining all of the important ideas.

On June 28, the committee presented Jefferson's rough draft of the Declaration of Independence to Congress. Most of the delegates liked the document. They wanted to make a decision about whether or not to declare independence, and they spent the next few days in debate. They recalled the words that Patrick Henry had said the year before in a passionate speech. He had stated, "Give me liberty or give me death!"

Finally, on July 2, the proposal to declare independence passed by a landslide. Jefferson's words had inspired the delegates. Although they knew it would be difficult and would require bloodshed, they wanted freedom. Then they could create a government unlike any ever seen before on Earth.

Comprehension Question

For what reasons did the congress decide to declare independence from Great Britain?

The American Revolution

It was April 1775. British General Thomas Gage went to Boston. He planned to find and take the guns that belonged to the colonists. He also wanted their gunpowder. The Sons of Liberty found out about this plan. Three men got on horses. Paul Revere was one of these men. The men rode in the dark. They told colonists that the British were coming. Some colonists got ready to fight in a few minutes. These men were called "minutemen."

The British soldiers met the colonists in Lexington, Massachusetts. No one knows who shot first. But it is called the "shot heard 'round the world." This shot began the American Revolution. Eight colonists died. One British soldier was hurt.

Important Battles

The British made General George Washington's leave from New York. Washington's army went to Pennsylvania. Washington wanted to catch the British off guard. He set out with 2,500 troops. It was Christmas Day 1776. They went across the river at night. The British soldiers did not know this. They were shocked when Washington's army showed up in Trenton, New Jersey. The colonists quickly took the town.

The Battle of Saratoga was very important. It changed the war. British General John Burgoyne crossed Lake Champlain. Then, he went down the Hudson River. He met the colonists in Saratoga, New York. The British troops fought hard. They fought for a month. Yet, the Americans won this battle.

France saw that the colonists could win. France and Great Britain did not like each other. So, France chose to help the Americans. They sent men to fight. They sent cash, too.

The War Ends

The last battle was at Yorktown, Virginia. General George Washington and the French navy blocked off the area. Then British General Charles Cornwallis was trapped. He could not get the things he needed. His men did not have enough food. His men did not have enough gunpowder. On October 11, 1781, the British gave up. The war ended. The colonists had done it. They were free!

British and American leaders went to France. They agreed to stop fighting. They made an agreement. It was called the Treaty of Paris. They signed it on September 3, 1783.

Comprehension Question

Why did France decide to help in the war?

The American Revolution

In April 1775, British General Thomas Gage went to Boston. He was to find and take the colonists' guns. He also wanted their gunpowder. The Sons of Liberty found out about his plan. Three men, including Paul Revere, got on horses and rode through the dark. They told the people that the British were coming. Colonists called "minutemen" got ready to fight. It took them just minutes to get ready.

The British soldiers and the colonists met in Lexington, Massachusetts. No one knows who fired the first shot. It is called the "shot heard 'round the world" because this battle started the American Revolution. Eight colonists were killed. Just one British soldier was hurt.

Important Battles

General George Washington decided to catch the British soldiers, or redcoats, off guard. The British had pushed his army back from New York to Pennsylvania. Washington set out with 2,500 troops. On Christmas Day 1776, they crossed the Delaware River at night. The British did not expect this. Washington's army landed in Trenton, New Jersey. They soon took over the city.

The Battle of Saratoga was the turning point of the war. British General John Burgoyne wanted to take Albany, New York. So, he crossed Lake Champlain. Then he went down the Hudson River. He met colonial fighters in Saratoga, New York. The British fought for a whole month. Still, they lost the fight. This showed France that the colonists could win. France and Britain had long been enemies. France chose to help the colonists. They sent money and soldiers.

The War Ends

The last big battle of the war was at Yorktown, Virginia. General George Washington and the French navy set up a blockade at Yorktown. This meant they closed off the area. British General Charles Cornwallis could not get supplies for his troops. The troops were running out of food. They were running out of gunpowder. On October 11, 1781, the British gave up. The war was over.

Later, a treaty was made. British and American leaders met in France. They signed the Treaty of Paris on September 3, 1783.

Comprehension Question

How did the French help the colonists in the war?

The American Revolution

In April 1775, British General Thomas Gage went to Boston. He was to find and take the colonists' guns and gunpowder. Paul Revere and the other Sons of Liberty found out his plan. Revere, William Dawes, and Samuel Prescott got on their horses and rode through the night. They told the colonists that the British were coming. Colonists called "minutemen" were ready to fight within minutes of getting these warnings.

The British soldiers and the colonial militia met in Lexington, Massachusetts. No one knows who fired the first shot. This is called the "shot heard 'round the world" because this battle started the American Revolution. Eight colonists were killed. Only one British soldier was hurt.

Important Battles

On Christmas Day 1776, General George Washington decided to catch the redcoats off guard. The British had pushed the Continental (kon-tuh-NEN-tuhl) Army back from New York to Pennsylvania. Washington set out with 2,500 troops. They crossed the Delaware River in the dark. The British did not expect them. When Washington's army landed in Trenton, New Jersey, they quickly took over the city.

Most people think of the Battle of Saratoga as the war's turning point. British General John Burgoyne wanted to take Albany, New York. So, he crossed Lake Champlain and traveled down the Hudson River. He met colonial fighters in Saratoga, New York. The British fought for an entire month, but they lost the battle. This victory by the colonial army showed France that the colonists could win. The British had long been enemies of the French. France decided to help the colonists. The French sent money and soldiers to help the Americans.

The War Ends

The last major battle of the war was at Yorktown, Virginia. General Washington and the French created a trap for British General Charles Cornwallis. The colonists and the French navy set up a blockade at Yorktown. This meant that Cornwallis was unable to get supplies. On October 11, 1781, he surrendered (suh-REN-duhrd) his armies. The war was over.

Later, a treaty was made between Britain and the colonists. The Treaty of Paris was signed in France on September 3, 1783.

Comprehension Question

How did France affect the outcome of the war?

The American Revolution

In April 1775, British General Thomas Gage was sent to Boston to locate and take possession of the colonists' stockpile of guns and gunpowder. Paul Revere and the other Sons of Liberty discovered his plan. Revere, William Dawes, and Samuel Prescott jumped on their horses. They rode through the night to warn the colonists that the British were coming. Colonists called "minutemen" were ready to fight within minutes of getting these warnings.

The British soldiers and the colonial militia met in Lexington, Massachusetts. Nobody knows who fired the first shot. This is called the "shot heard 'round the world" because this battle started the American Revolution. Eight colonists were killed, while only one British soldier was injured.

Important Battles

On Christmas Day 1776, General George Washington made a major move to catch the redcoats off guard. The British had pushed the Continental (kon-tuh-NEN-tuhl) Army back from New York to Pennsylvania. Washington set out with 2,500 troops. They crossed the Delaware River under cover of darkness. The British were not expecting them. When Washington's army landed in Trenton, New Jersey, they quickly captured the city.

Most people think of the Battle of Saratoga as the war's turning point. British General John Burgoyne wanted to capture Albany, New York, so he crossed Lake Champlain and traveled down the Hudson River. He met colonial fighters in Saratoga, New York. The British fought for an entire month but lost the battle. This important victory by the colonial army showed France that the colonists could win the war. The British had long been enemies of the French. France decided to help the colonists. The French sent money and soldiers to assist the Americans.

The War Ends

The last major battle of the war was at Yorktown, Virginia, on October 11, 1781. General Washington and the French decided to create a trap for British General Charles Cornwallis. The colonists and the French navy set up a blockade at Yorktown, and Cornwallis was unable to get necessary supplies. He surrendered (suh-REN-duhrd) his armies. The war was over.

Afterwards, a treaty was made between Great Britain and the colonists. The Treaty of Paris was signed in France on September 3, 1783.

Comprehension Question

In what ways did France change the course of the war?

Early Congresses

Before America became a nation, no one knew that people could make their own laws. Everyone thought that just kings or queens could rule. They did not think that common people could be in charge. A group of smart, brave men changed all that. They lived in the colonies. They formed the first congresses. They formed a new kind of government. It let people make their own choices.

Declaring Freedom

In the year 1774, the First Continental (kon-tuh-NEN-tuhl) Congress met. Some of the men wanted to go to war against Great Britain. Others said that they should find a way to work with Great Britain. Congress sent a letter to King George III. It told how the people felt about taxes and their lack of rights. The men agreed to meet seven months later. Then, they would talk about what the king said. But the king did not respond.

The Second Continental Congress met. They had to make a choice. Would the colony stay a part of Great Britain or not? The colonists and the British soldiers had started fighting. But, being free from Great Britain was still a big step. Some men wanted to give the king one more chance. They did not want a war. So, they sent a new letter. It asked the king to get rid of the unfair taxes. It said that the colonists would be glad if he did. The king did nothing.

The men talked about what to do next. They talked again and again. At last, on July 2, 1776, the Congress approved the Declaration of Independence. The men signed it on July 4. They risked their lives to do so. The king was mad. He made it a point to go after these men.

Setting Up the Government

In November 1777, another congress met. This group wrote the Articles of Confederation (kuhn-fed-er-RAY-shuhn). These laws set up the first government. But, it did not give real power to anyone. Over time people saw that the Articles of Confederation did not work.

Then, the Constitutional (kon-stuh-TOO-shuhn-uhl) Convention met. These men wrote a new document. It was the Constitution. It set up three parts of government. The congress, the president, and the courts would share power. One branch would not be stronger than another.

Comprehension Question

What were the three parts of the new government?

Early Congresses

Before America became a nation, no one knew that common people could make their own laws. Most people thought that only priests, kings or queens could rule. They did not think that people could govern themselves. A group of smart, brave men in the colonies changed that way of thinking. They formed the first congresses. They took the first steps toward a government where common people made their own choices.

Declaring Independence

The First Continental (kon-tuh-NEN-tuhl) Congress met in 1774. Some of the men thought it was best to declare war against Great Britain. Others said that they should try to work things out. Congress sent a letter to King George III. It was called the Declaration of Rights and Grievances (GREE-vuhn-zez). It told how the people felt about taxes and their lack of rights. The men agreed to meet seven months later. Then, they would talk about the king's response. But, the king ignored the letter.

The Second Continental Congress met as planned. They had to make a big decision. The colonists and the British soldiers had started fighting. Still, breaking free from Great Britain was a big step. Some of the men wanted to give the king one last chance. They did not want a war. So, they wrote a letter. It was called the Olive Branch Petition (peh-TISH-uhn). It asked the king to get rid of the unfair taxes. It also said that the colonists would stop protesting if he did. Once again, the king did not respond.

The men talked about what to do next. At last, on July 2, 1776, Congress approved the Declaration of Independence. The men signed it on July 4. They risked their lives to do so. The king was mad. He made it a point to go after the signers.

Setting Up the Government

In November 1777, another Congress met. It wrote the Articles of Confederation (kuhn-fed-er-RAY-shuhn). These laws served as the first constitution of the United States. But, this document did not give real power to anyone. Over time people saw that the Articles of Confederation were not working.

A Constitutional (kon-stuh-TOO-shuhn-uhl) Convention was held. These men wrote a document called the Constitution. It set up three branches of government. This way, Congress, the president, and the court system would share power. No branch of government would be stronger than another.

Comprehension Question

Describe the government set up by the colonists.

Early Congresses

Before America became a nation, no one thought that common people could make their own laws or govern themselves. People believed that only priests or royalty were fit to rule. A group of brave, brilliant men changed that way of thinking. They formed the first congresses in the colonies. They took the first steps toward a government in which common people made their own choices.

Declaring Independence

The First Continental (kon-tuh-NEN-tuhl) Congress met in Philadelphia in 1774. Some of the delegates thought it was best to declare war against Great Britain. Others believed they should try to work things out. Congress sent a letter called the Declaration of Rights and Grievances to King George III. It explained how the people felt about taxes and their lack of rights. The delegates agreed to meet seven months later to discuss the king's response. The king ignored the letter.

The Second Continental Congress met as planned. They had to make a big decision. The colonists and the British soldiers had already started fighting. Still, declaring independence from Great Britain was a big step. There were some men who wanted to give the king one last chance. They wanted to avoid a long, brutal war. So, they wrote a letter called the Olive Branch Petition (peh-TISH-uhn). It asked the king to cancel the unfair tax laws. It also promised that the protests would stop if the king met their demands. Once again, the king ignored the letter.

The delegates argued about what to do next. At last, on July 2, 1776, Congress approved the Declaration of Independence. The delegates signed it on July 4. They risked their lives to do so. The king was mad. He made it a point to go after the signers.

Setting Up the Government

In November 1777, Congress wrote the Articles of Confederation (kuhn-fed-er-RAY-shuhn). Once they were approved, these laws served as the first constitution of the United States. However, this document did not give much power to anyone, and over time people realized that the Articles of Confederation were not working.

A Constitutional (kon-stuh-TOO-shuhn-uhl) Convention was held. These delegates prepared a document called the Constitution. It set up three branches of government. This made it so that Congress, the president, and the court system would share power.

Comprehension Question

Tell how the colonists wanted the government to work.

Early Congresses

Before America became a nation, nobody thought that ordinary people could make their own laws or govern themselves. People believed that only priests or royalty were fit to rule. A group of brave, brilliant men changed that way of thinking by forming the first congresses in the colonies. They took the first steps toward a government in which common people made their own choices.

Declaring Independence

The First Continental (kon-tuh-NEN-tuhl) Congress met in Philadelphia in 1774. Some of the delegates thought it was best to break away and declare war, while others believed they should try to work with Great Britain. Congress wrote a letter called the Declaration of Rights and Grievances and sent it to King George III to explain how they felt about taxes and their lack of rights. The delegates agreed to meet seven months later to hear the king's response, but the king completely ignored the letter.

The Second Continental Congress met as planned. They had important decisions to make. The colonists and the British soldiers had already started fighting. Still, declaring independence from Great Britain was a big step. There were some men who wanted to give the king one last chance to avoid a long, brutal war. So, they wrote a letter called the Olive Branch Petition (peh-TISH-uhn). It asked the king to repeal, or cancel, the unfair tax laws and promised that the protests would stop if he met their demands. Once again, the king ignored their requests.

The delegates debated what to do next. Finally, on July 2, 1776, Congress approved the Declaration of Independence, and the delegates signed it on July 4. They risked their lives to do so. The king was angry with anyone involved in creating that document.

Setting Up the Government

In November 1777, Congress wrote the Articles of Confederation (kuhn-fed-er-RAY-shuhn). Once they were ratified, or approved, these articles served as the first constitution of the United States. However, this document did not give much power to anyone. Over time, people realized that the Articles of Confederation were not working. Thus, a Constitutional (kon-stuh-TOO-shuhn-uhl) Convention was held in which a document called the Constitution was prepared. It set up three branches of government that shared power: a congress, a president, and a court system.

Comprehension Question

In what ways was the American government different from other governments?

The Constitution of the United States

The United States Constitution is an important document. It tells how the government works. The government has three parts, or branches. There is the legislative (LEJ-is-lay-tiv) branch. There is the executive (eg-ZEK-yoo-tiv) branch. And, there is the judicial (joo-DISH-uhl) branch. Each part has its own job. Each branch has the same amount of power.

The new Americans did not want one branch to be too strong. The British king had used his power against them. They did not want that to happen again. That is why all three parts share power.

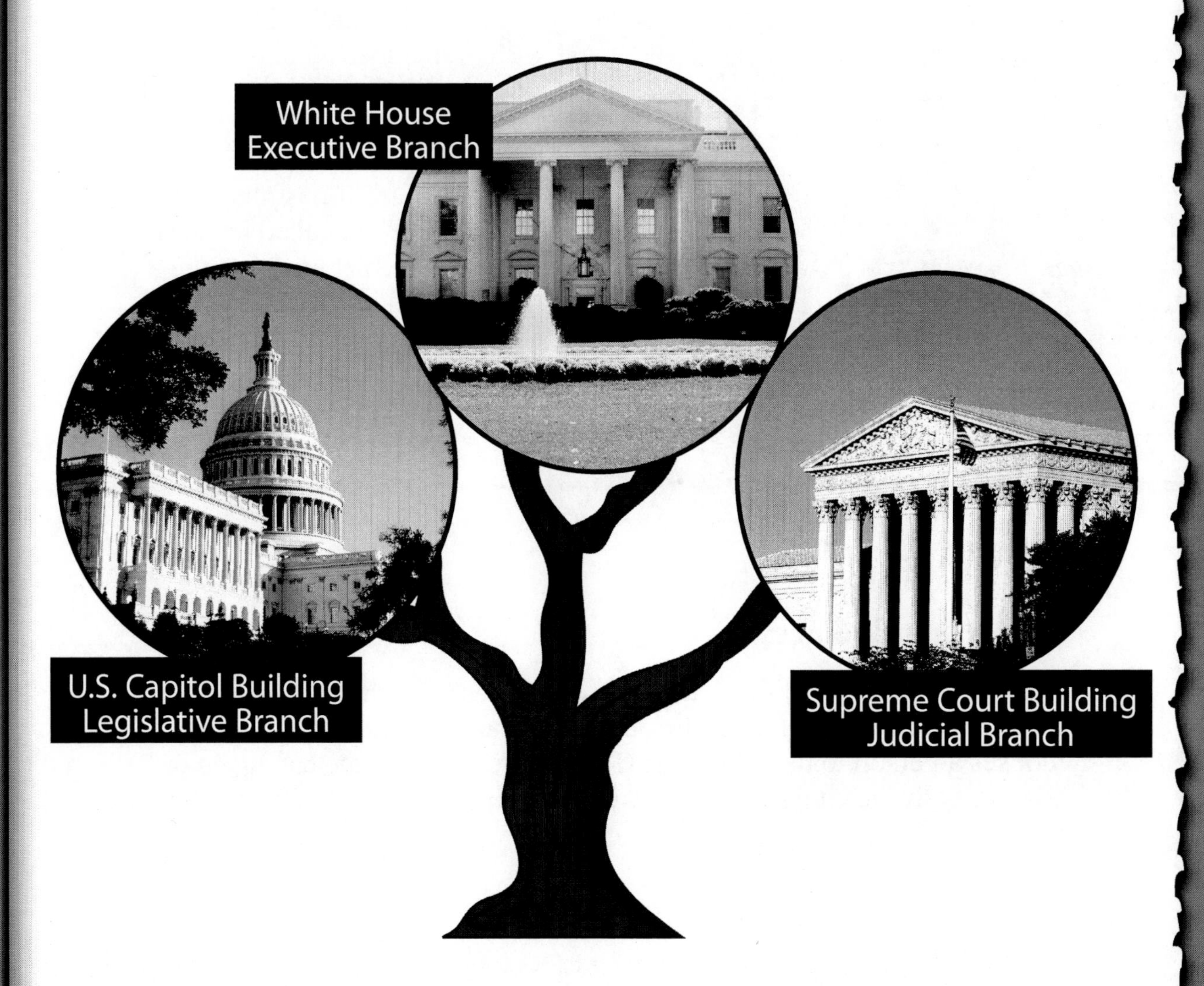

Three Equal Branches

The legislative branch makes the nation's laws. It is made up of the members of Congress. The Congress has two parts. They are the Senate and the House of Representatives (rep-rih-ZEN-tuh-tivs). Each state has two senators in the Senate. The House of Representatives is different. The number of representatives from each state is based on how many people live there. States with more people have more representatives in Congress than states with fewer people.

The executive branch carries out the laws. The president is the head of this branch. He picks a group of people. They form his cabinet. They help him. There are rules for who can be the president. The person must be at least 35 years old. The person must have been born a citizen of the United States. He or she must have lived in the nation for at least 14 years.

The judicial branch includes all of the nation's courts. The courts decide what the laws mean. The highest court is the Supreme Court. It has nine judges. They are called justices. The chief justice is the head judge. Being part of this court is a great honor. These judges are chosen for life.

Checks and Balances

The Constitution set up "checks and balances." Each branch must do its job. And, it must watch over the other branches. For example, the president chooses a person to be a Supreme Court judge. The Senate can agree or disagree with the choice. In this way, the branches "check" each other.

Comprehension Question

Describe in detail one of the branches of the government.

The Constitution of the United States

The United States Constitution tells how the nation's government works. The government has three parts. They are called branches. Each branch has a different job. Each branch has the same amount of power. The new Americans wanted to be sure that one branch could not be too strong. The British king had used his power against them. They did not want that to happen in their new government. As a result, the Constitution's writers split the government into three branches. They are the legislative (LEJ-is-lay-tiv), executive (eg-ZEK-yoo-tiv), and judicial (joo-DISH-uhl) branches.

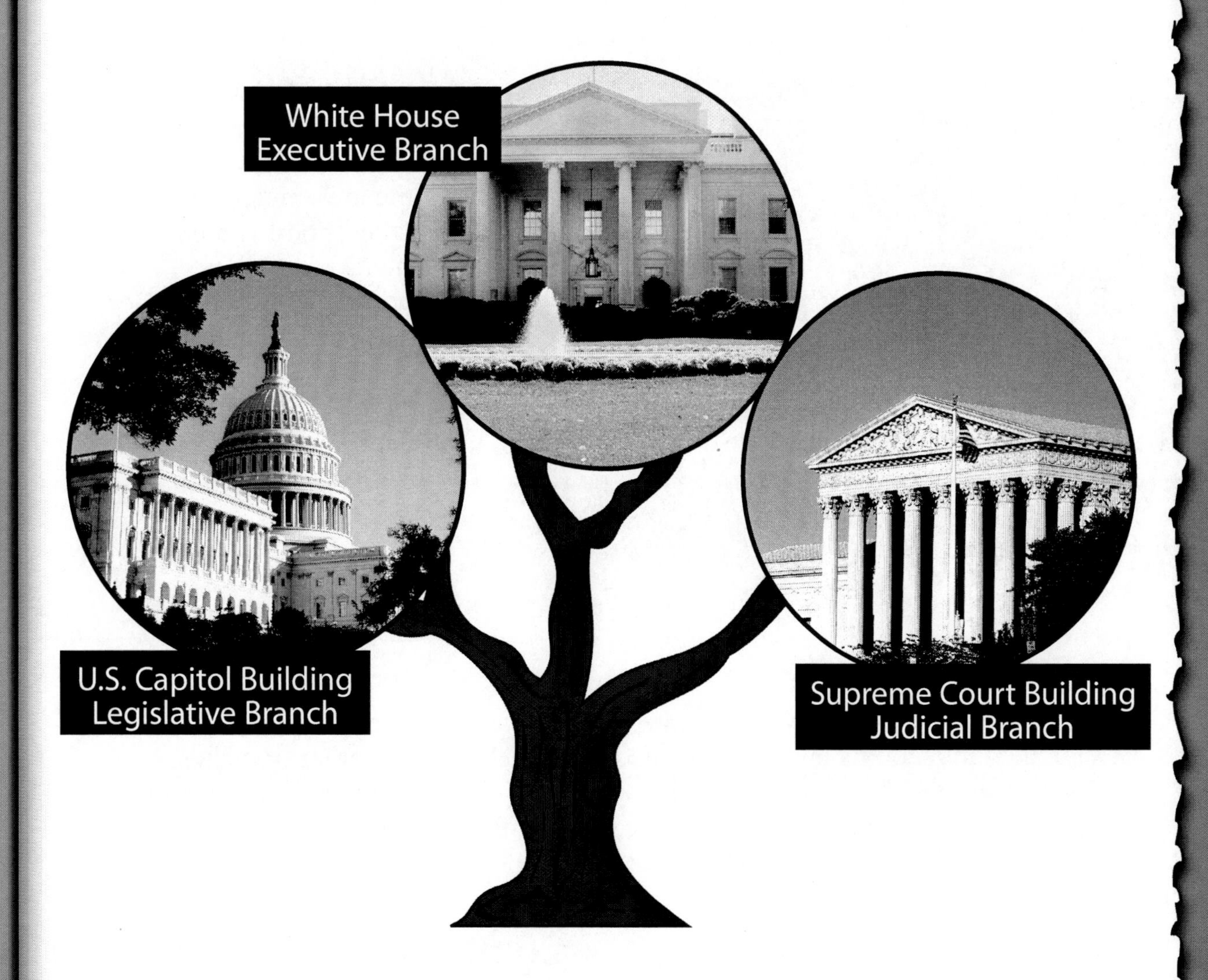

Three Equal Branches

The legislative branch makes the nation's laws. This branch is made up of the members of Congress. The members of the Senate and the House of Representatives (rep-rih-ZEN-tuh-tivs) form the Congress. Every state has two senators. So, every state is equally represented when laws are created in the Senate. In the House of Representatives, the number of representatives from each state is based on how many people live in the state. States with more people have more representatives in Congress.

The executive branch enforces the laws. The president is the head of this branch. He picks a group of people. They form his cabinet. They help him. The Constitution has rules about who can be the president. The person must be at least 35 years old. The person must have been born a citizen of the United States. He or she must have lived in the country for at least 14 years.

The judicial branch includes all of the nation's courts. The courts decide what the laws mean. The highest court is the Supreme Court. It has nine judges. They are called justices. The chief justice is in charge. Being picked for the Supreme Court is a great honor. These judges are chosen for life.

Checks and Balances

The Constitution's writers created "checks and balances." Each branch must do its own job. It must also watch over the other branches. For example, the president nominates, or suggests, a Supreme Court justice. The Senate must then agree or disagree. This is one way in which the branches "check" each other.

Comprehension Question

How do the branches work together?

The Constitution of the United States

The Constitution of the United States tells how the nation's government works. The government has three parts. Each part has a different job but the same amount of power. The new Americans wanted to be sure that one branch could not be too strong. The king of Great Britain had used his power against them. They did not want that to happen in their new government. As a result, the Constitution's writers divided the government into the legislative (LEJ-is-lay-tiv), executive (eg-ZEK-yoo-tiv), and judicial (joo-DISH-uhl) branches. They felt that three branches were necessary.

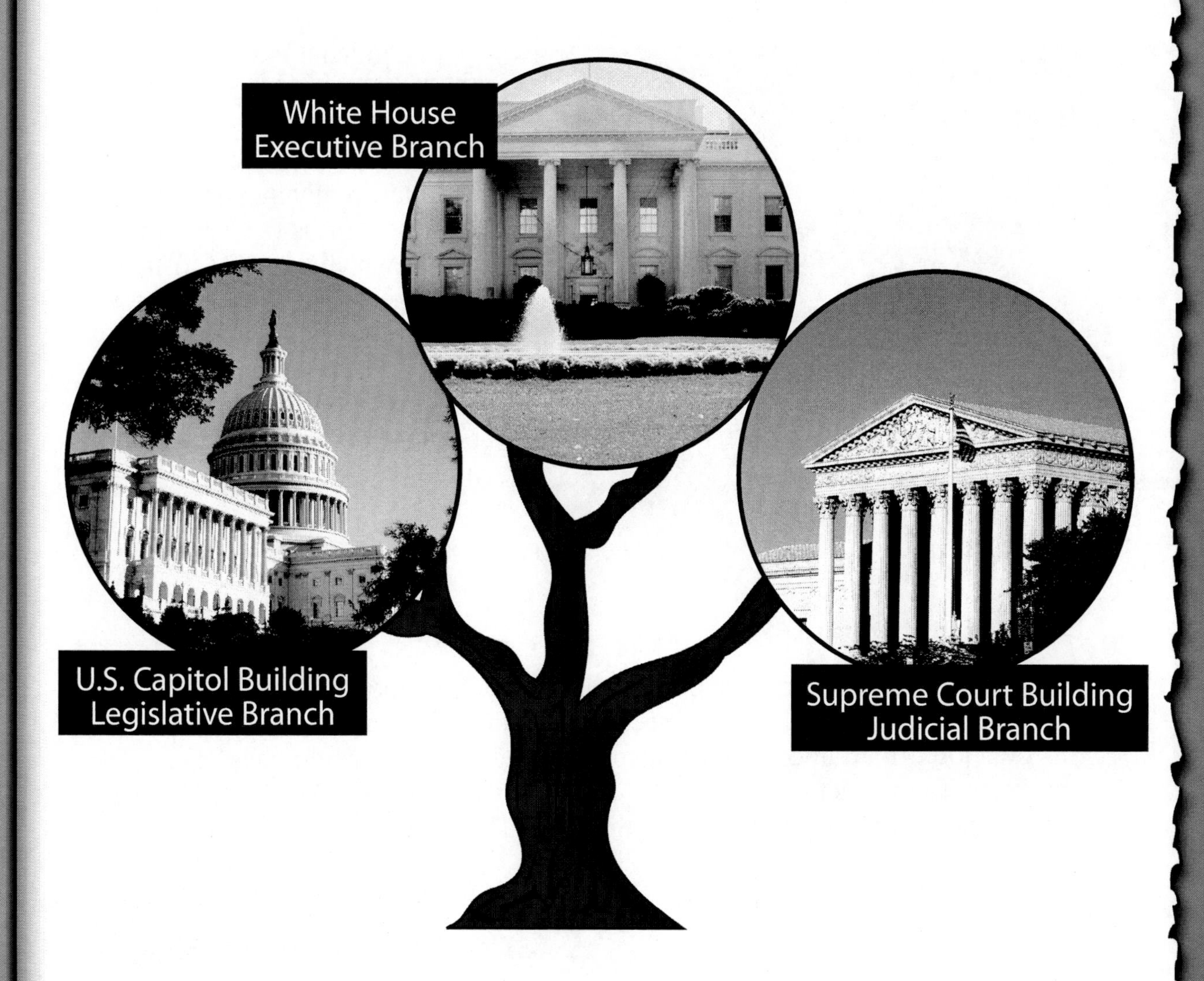

Three Equal Branches

The legislative branch makes the country's laws. This branch is made up of the members of Congress. The members of the Senate and the House of Representatives (rep-rih-ZEN-tuh-tivs) form the Congress. Every state has two senators, which means that every state is equally represented when laws are created in the Senate. In the House of Representatives, the number of representatives from each state depends on the state's population. States with more people have more representatives in Congress than states with fewer people.

The executive branch enforces the laws. The president is the head of this branch. He appoints a group of people to his cabinet to be his assistants. The Constitution states rules about who can become president. The candidate must be at least 35 years old, born a citizen of the United States, and have lived in the country for at least 14 years.

The judicial branch includes all of the nation's courts. The courts interpret laws. This means that they decide what each law really means. The highest court is the Supreme Court, which has nine justices, or judges. The chief justice is the one in charge. Being picked for the Supreme Court is a great honor, especially because these justices are appointed for life.

Checks and Balances

To ensure that no one person or group could have too much power, the Constitution's writers created "checks and balances." Each branch must do its own job. In addition, it must also watch over the other branches. For example, the president nominates a Supreme Court justice. The Senate must then agree or disagree with the nomination. This is one way in which the branches "check" each other.

Comprehension Question

Why did the Americans worry about one branch being too strong?

The Constitution of the United States

The Constitution of the United States explains how the nation's government works. The government has three parts—each with a different job but the same amount of power. The new Americans wanted to ensure that one branch could not become too strong. The king of Great Britain had used his power against them. They wanted to prevent that from happening in their new government. Therefore, the Constitution's writers divided the government into the legislative (LEJ-is-lay-tiv), executive (eg-ZEK-yoo-tiv), and judicial (joo-DISH-uhl) branches. They felt that three branches were necessary for a balanced system.

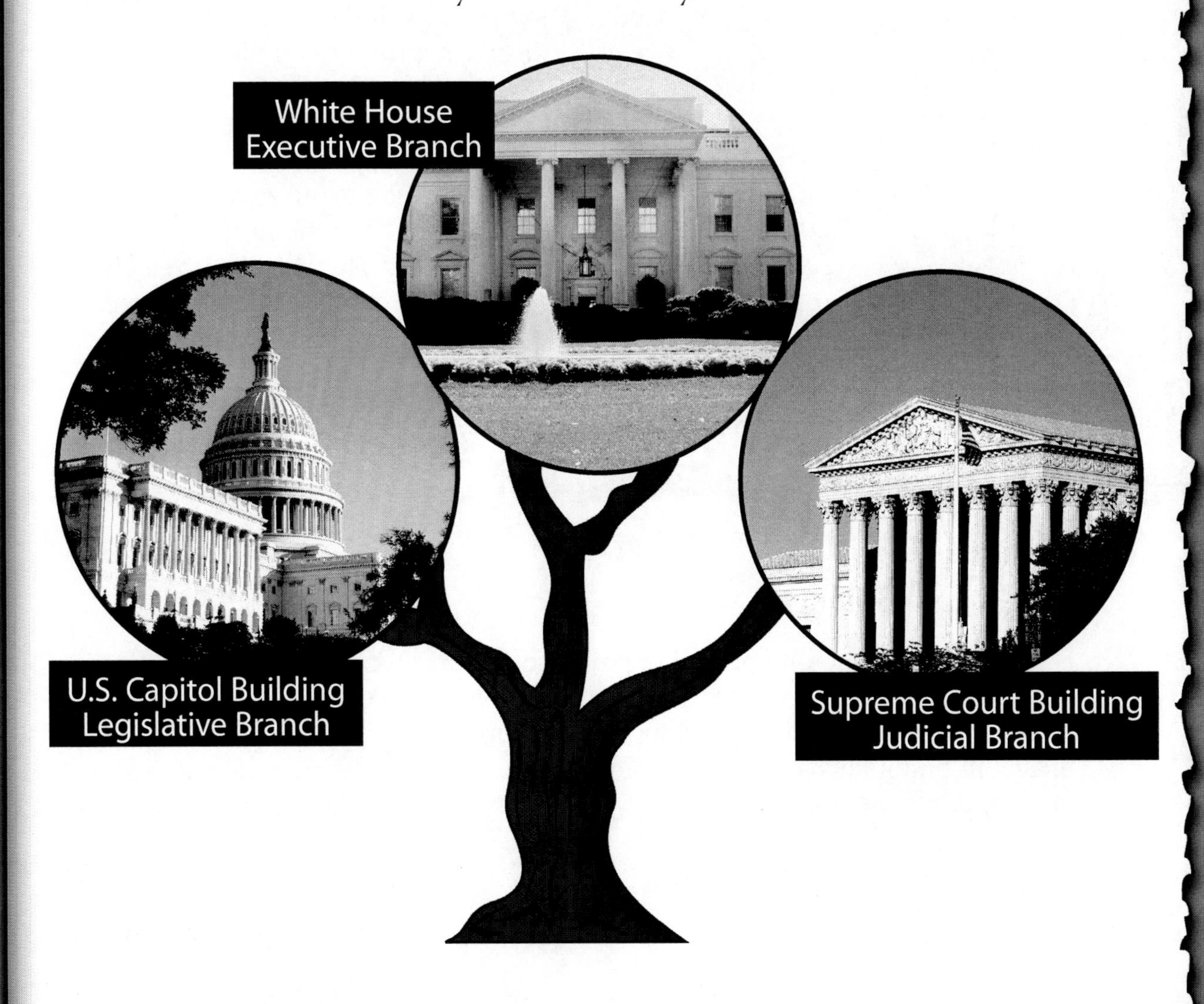

Three Equal Branches

The legislative branch creates the country's laws. This branch is made up of the members of Congress, which is formed by the House of Representatives (rep-rih-ZEN-tuh-tivs) and the Senate. Every state has two senators, which means that every state is equally represented when laws are created in the Senate. In the House of Representatives, the number of representatives from each state depends on the state's population. More populous states have more representatives than less populous states.

The executive branch enforces the laws. The president is the head of this branch, and he appoints a group of people to his cabinet to be his assistants. The Constitution states specific rules about who can become president. The candidate must be at least 35 years old, born a citizen of the United States, and have lived in the country for at least 14 years.

The judicial branch is comprised of all the nation's courts. The courts interpret laws by deciding what each one really means. The highest court is the Supreme Court, which has nine justices, or judges. The chief justice is the one in charge. Being selected for the Supreme Court is a great honor, especially because these justices are appointed for life.

Checks and Balances

To ensure that no one person or group could have too much power, the Constitution's writers created "checks and balances." Each branch must do its own job, in addition to watching over the other branches. For example, the president nominates a Supreme Court justice. The Senate must then approve or disapprove the nomination. This is one way in which the branches "check" each other.

Comprehension Question

What could happen if one branch of government had more power than the other branches?

The Bill of Rights

When the Constitution was written, people were upset. They remembered when the king had too much control over them. They wanted to avoid this abuse of power. The colonists wanted a new kind of government. They had fought a war to have it.

Some of the men did not like the Constitution. It did not list the people's rights. The men were afraid. They thought that the government could abuse people. Virginia had a bill of rights. Many people felt that a bill of rights must be in the United States Constitution, too.

In the year 1791, the Bill of Rights was added. It is the first ten amendments to the Constitution. The word *amendments* means changes. The Constitution has had many amendments over the years.

People Have Rights

The Bill of Rights protects each American. It tells the people that the government cannot hurt them. The First Amendment says that a person can have any religion. Or, a person can have no religion. Also, people can say what they want. They do not have to agree with leaders. They can talk against a leader. The leader cannot hurt them. The leader cannot put them in jail. They do not have to be afraid. This is not true in many nations, even today.

Newspapers can choose what to print. People can meet. They can speak against things. They can say things must change. No one can stop them. This is not true in many nations.

The Fifth Amendment protects those charged with a crime. It says that each person will get a trial. A person is "innocent until proven guilty." A person cannot be tried twice for the same crime. A person does not have to speak at his or her own trial.

Both the United States Constitution and the Bill of Rights are strong documents. The Constitution does not let the government have too much power. The Bill of Rights gives each person rights. Both show the value of freedom.

Comprehension Question

What is the Bill of Rights?

We the People

Article 1

Congress of the United States

The Bill of Rights

When the Constitution was written, people did not want the government to be too powerful. The British king had had too much control over them when they were colonists. They wanted to avoid this in the new government.

Some of the men did not like the Constitution. It did not list the people's rights. The men were afraid. They thought that the government could abuse its power. George Mason had written a bill of rights for Virginia. He thought that a bill of rights should be part of the United States Constitution, too.

The Bill of Rights was added in the year 1791. It is the first ten amendments to the Constitution. Amendments are changes.

People Have Rights

The Bill of Rights protects the rights of each American. They tell the people that the government cannot abuse them. Some people think the First Amendment is the most important amendment. It states that an American can have any religion. If a person wants to, he or she can have no religion at all. People can say what they want. They can disagree with leaders. They do not have to be afraid.

Newspapers can decide what to print. People can hold meetings. They can talk about the nation's problems. They can speak against things that they think are wrong. The government cannot stop them.

The Fifth Amendment protects people accused of a crime. It states that each person will get a trial. Each person is "innocent until proven guilty." A person cannot be tried for the same crime twice. Also, a person does not have to speak at his or her own trial.

The United States Constitution and the Bill of Rights are strong documents. Each one gives people important protections. The Constitution keeps the government from having too much power. The Bill of Rights states each person's rights. Both show the importance of freedom to all Americans.

Comprehension Question

How does the Bill of Rights protect Americans?

We the People

Article. I

Congress of the United States

The Bill of Rights

When the Constitution was being written, many people wanted to be sure that the government did not get too much power. They kept remembering Great Britain's control over them when they were colonists.

Some of the men were upset by the final document. The rights of the people were not stated. They feared that the federal government could abuse its power. George Mason cried, "It has no declaration of rights!" Mason had written a bill of rights for the state of Virginia. He wanted one included in the United States Constitution, too.

The Bill of Rights was added in the year 1791. The Bill of Rights is the first ten amendments, or changes, to the Constitution.

Individuals' Rights

The Bill of Rights is so named because these amendments protect the rights of all Americans. They tell the people that the government cannot abuse them.

Many people think the First Amendment is the most important. It states that Americans can have any religion they want, or they can chose to have no religion at all. Americans can say what they want. They do not have to be afraid of arrest if they do not agree with leaders. Newspapers and magazines can decide what to print. People can meet together peacefully. They can talk about the nation's problems. They can protest things that they think are wrong. The government cannot stop any of this.

The Fifth Amendment protects people who have been accused of a crime. It states that each accused person will have a trial before being called guilty. Each person is "innocent until proven guilty." A person cannot be tried for the same crime twice. Also, a person does not have to speak at his or her own trial.

The United States Constitution and the Bill of Rights are powerful documents. Each one gives Americans protection. The Constitution ensures that no branch of government has too much power. The Bill of Rights gives rights to each individual. Both show the importance of freedom to all Americans.

Comprehension Question

Describe at least three ways the Bill of Rights protects Americans.

The Bill of Rights

When the Constitution was being written, many delegates wanted to ensure that the government did not get too much power over individuals. They kept remembering Great Britain's control over them when they were colonists.

Some of the delegates were upset by the final document because the rights of the people were not specifically stated. They feared that the federal government could abuse its power. George Mason cried, "It has no declaration of rights!" Mason had written a bill of rights in the Virginia Constitution. He wanted a bill of rights included in the United States Constitution.

The Bill of Rights was added to the Constitution in 1791. The Bill of Rights is the first ten amendments, or changes, to the Constitution.

Individuals' Rights

The Bill of Rights is so named because these amendments protect the rights of all Americans. These amendments (as well as others) tell the people that the government cannot abuse them.

Many people think the First Amendment is the most important amendment. It states that Americans can practice any religion they want, or they can choose to have no religious beliefs at all. Americans can say what they want without having to be afraid of arrest or imprisonment. Newspapers and magazines can decide what stories to print. People can meet together peacefully and talk about the country's problems. They can protest things that they think are wrong. The government cannot stop any of this.

The Fifth Amendment protects people who have been arrested. It guarantees that each accused person will have a trial before being labeled guilty. Each person is "innocent until proven guilty." A person cannot be tried for the same crime twice. Also, nobody can be forced to speak at his or her own trial.

The United States Constitution and the Bill of Rights are powerful documents, and each one provides Americans with essential protections. The Constitution ensures that no branch of government has too much power. The Bill of Rights gives personal rights to each individual. Both show how important freedom is to all Americans.

Comprehension Question

For what reasons did Americans think it was necessary to have the Bill of Rights?

Resources

Works Cited

August, Diane and Timothy Shanahan (Eds). (2006). *Developing literacy in second-language learners: Report of the National Literacy Panel on language-minority children and youth.* Mahwah, NJ: Lawrence Erlbaum Associates, Inc.

Marzano, Robert, Debra Pickering, and Jane Pollock. (2001). *Classroom instruction that works.* Alexandria, VA: Association for Supervision and Curriculum Development.

Tomlinson, Carol Ann. (2000). Leadership for Differentiating Schools and Classrooms, Alexandria, VA: Association for Supervision and Curriculum Development.

Image Sources

Page	Description	Photo Credit/Source	Filename
21, 23, 25, 27, (top)	Map of the Americas with portraits of Columbus, Vespucci, Magellan, and Pizarro	The Library of Congress, Prints and Photographs Division. Washington, D.C. (LC-USZ62-89908)	newworld.jpg
21, 23, 25, 27, (bottom)	Nina, Pinta, and Santa Maria	Clipart.com (838883)	ships.jpg
22, 24, 26, 28, (top)	Henry Hudson's crew in mutiny	Clipart.com (802057)	mutiny.jpg
22, 24, 26, 28, (bottom)	Map of Columbus voyage	Historical Documents Co.	voyage.jpg
29, 31, 33, 35, (top)	Viking boat	J. Helgasod/Shutterstock, Inc. (1077695)	viking.jpg
29, 31, 33, 35, (bottom)	Christopher Columbus meeting King Ferdinand and Queen Isabella	The Library of Congress, Prints and Photographs Division. Washington, D.C. (LC-USZC2-3750)	columbus.jpg
30, 32, 34, 36, (top)	Martin Waldseemuller's map	The Library of Congress, Geography and Map Division. Washington, D.C. (G3200 1507.W3 Vault)	waldseem.jpg
30, 32, 34, 36, (bottom)	Amerigo Vespucci fighting the Amazons	Clipart.com (53732)	vespucci.jpg
37, 39, 41, 43, (top)	Indian village with birch bark wigwams	The Library of Congress, Prints and Photographs Division. Washington, D.C. (LC-USZ62-106105)	wigwam.jpg
37, 39, 41, 43, (middle)	Map of regional tribe areas	Teacher Created Materials	northest.jpg
38, 40, 42, 44, (top)	Map of regional tribe areas	Teacher Created Materials	southest.jpg
38, 40, 42, 44, (bottom)	Seminole Indians in front of chickees	The Library of Congress, Prints and Photographs Division. Washington, D.C. (LC-USZ62-104529)	chickees.jpg
45, 47, 49, 51, (top)	Map of regional tribe areas	Teacher Created Materials	plains.jpg
45, 47, 49, 51, (middle)	Wichita grass house	The Library of Congress, Prints and Photographs Division. Washington, D.C. (LC-USZ62-118773)	wichita.jpg
45, 47, 49, 51, (bottom left)	Mandan earth lodge	The Library of Congress, Prints and Photographs Division. Washington, D.C. (LC-USZ62-114582)	mandan.jpg

Resources *(cont.)*

Image Sources *(cont.)*

Page	Description	Photo Credit/Source	Filename
45, 47, 49, 51, (bottom right)	Dakota tepee	The National Archives, College Park, MD (NWDNS-75-BAE-1448D; Record Group 75)	tepee.jpg
46, 48, 50, 52, (top)	Sioux Sun Dance ceremony	The Library of Congress, Prints and Photographs Division. Washington, D.C. (LC-USZ62-117138)	sioux.jpg
46, 48, 50, 52, (bottom)	Bison	The Library of Congress, Prints and Photographs Division. Washington, D.C. (LC-USZC4-2629)	bison.jpg
53, 55, 57, 59, (top)	Map of regional tribe areas	Teacher Created Materials	southwst.jpg
53, 55, 57, 59, (middle)	Navajo weaver	The National Archives, Anchorage, AK (NRIS-75-PAO50-NAVRUG11; Record Group 75)	weaver.jpg
53, 55, 57, 59, (bottom)	American Indian vase	Greg A. Bolarsky/Shutterstock, Inc. (1105491)	vase.jpg
54, 56, 58, 60, (top)	Map of regional tribe areas	Teacher Created Materials	northwst.jpg
54, 56, 58, 60, (bottom)	Indian women cleaning a beluga whale	The Library of Congress, Prints and Photographs Division. Washington, D.C., (LC-USZ62-115975)	whale.jpg
61, 63, 65, 67, (top)	Boston Harbor	The Library of Congress, Prints and Photographs Division. Washington, D.C. (LC-USZ62-45537)	boston.jpg
61, 63, 65, 67, (bottom)	Roger Williams	Clipart.com (335029)	puritan.jpg
62, 64, 66, 68	Cod fishing in New England	The Library of Congress, Prints and Photographs Division. Washington, D.C. (LC-USZC2-2116)	fishing.jpg
69, 71, 73, 75	The British take over New Netherland	The Library of Congress, Prints and Photographs Division. Washington, D.C. (LC-USZ62-84401)	nthrland.jpg
70, 72, 74, 76, (top)	Philadelphia in the 1700s	The Library of Congress, Prints and Photographs Division. Washington, D.C. (LC-USZ62-3282)	ports.jpg
70, 72, 74, 76, (bottom)	Colonial farm near Baltimore, Maryland	The Library of Congress, Rare Book and Special Collections Division. Washington, D.C. (LC-USZ62-31149)	farm.jpg
77, 79, 81, 83	The first British colonists building Jamestown	Clipart.com (391051)	jamestwn.jpg
78, 80, 82, 84, (top)	Rice farming in Georgia	The Library of Congress, Prints and Photographs Division. Washington, D.C. (LC-USZ62-93554)	ricefarm.jpg
78, 80, 82, 84, (bottom)	Church in Jamestown	Courtesy of Emily Smith	church.jpg
85, 87, 89, 91	Slaves being brought to the colonies	The Library of Congress, Prints and Photographs Division. Washington, D.C. (LC-USZ62-41678)	slavery.jpg

Resources *(cont.)*

Image Sources *(cont.)*

Page	Description	Photo Credit/Source	Filename
86, 88, 90, 92, (top)	Map of Africa	The Library of Congress, Geography and Map Division. Washington, D.C. (G8200 1688.W5 TIL Vault)	africa.jpg
86, 88, 90, 92, (bottom)	Phillis Wheatley	The Library of Congress, Prints and Photographs Division. Washington, D.C. (LC-USZC4-5316)	wheatley.jpg
93, 95, 97, 99, (left)	British Tax Stamp	Dover Publications, American Revolution: A Picture Sourcebook, John Grafton	taxstamp.jpg
93, 95, 97, 99, (right)	Protest of the Stamp Act	The Library of Congress, Prints and Photographs Division. Washington, D.C. (LC-USZ61-449)	protest.jpg
94, 96, 98, 100	Paul Revere's engraving of the Boston Massacre	The National Archives, College Park, MD (NWDNS-111-SC-92632; Record Group 111)	massacre.jpg
101, 103, 105, 107	The Declaration of Independence committee	The Library of Congress, Prints and Photographs Division. Washington, D.C. (LC-USZC2-2243)	commitee.jpg
102, 104, 106, 108, (top)	Writing the Declaration of Independence	The Library of Congress, Prints and Photographs Division. Washington, D.C. (LC-USZC4-9904)	writing.jpg
102, 104, 106, 108, (bottom)	The first reading of the Declaration of Independence	The Library of Congress, Prints and Photographs Division. Washington, D.C. (LC-USZC4-2485)	reading.jpg
109, 111, 113, 115	Paul Revere's ride	The National Archives, College Park, MD (NWDNS-208-FS-3200-5; Record Group 208)	revere.jpg
110, 112, 114, 116, (top)	Washington crossing the Delaware River on December 25, 1776	The Library of Congress, Prints and Photographs Division. Washington, D.C. (LC-USZC2-3156)	delaware.jpg
110, 112, 114, 116, (bottom)	Washington with officers of the Colonial Army	The Library of Congress, Prints and Photographs Division. Washington, D.C. (LC-USZC4-3359)	washngtn.jpg
117, 119, 121, 123	The meeting of the Continental Congress	The Library of Congress, Prints and Photographs Division. Washington, D.C. (LC-USZ62-45328)	congress.jpg
118, 120, 122, 124	Leaders of the Continental Congress	The Library of Congress, Prints and Photographs Division. Washington, D.C. (LC-USZC4-7216)	leaders.jpg
125, 127, 129, 131,	Three branches of U.S. government	Jim Steinhart/www.TravelPhotoBase.com	branches.jpg
126, 128, 130, 132	The nine justices of the Supreme Court in 1888	The Library of Congress, Prints and Photographs Division. Washington, D.C. (LC-USZ62-90608)	supcourt.jpg
133, 135, 137, 139	The United States Constitution and the Bill of Rights	The National Archives, College Park, MD (Record Group 360) and (Record Group 11)	documnts.jpg
134, 136, 138, 140	March on Washington, 1963	The National Archives, College Park, MD (NWDNS-306-SSM-4C(35) 6; Record Group 306)	march.jpg

Resources *(cont.)*

Contents of Teacher Resource CD

PDF Files

The full-color pdfs provided are each eight pages long and contain all four levels of a reading passage. For example, Exploring the New World PDF (pages 21–28) is the *explore1.pdf* file.

Text Files

The *Microsoft Word* documents include the text for all four levels of each reading passage. For example, Exploring the New World text (pages 21–28) is the *explore1.doc* file.

Text Title	Text File	PDF
Exploring the New World	explore1.doc	explore1.pdf
Explorers	explore2.doc	explore2.pdf
American Indian Tribes of the East	east.doc	east.pdf
American Indian Tribes of the Plains	plains.doc	plains.pdf
American Indian Tribes of the West	west.doc	west.pdf
The New England Colonies	north.doc	north.pdf
The Middle Colonies	middle.doc	middle.pdf
The Southern Colonies	south.doc	south.pdf
Slavery in the New World	slavery.doc	slavery.pdf
Causes of the American Revolution	revoltn1.doc	revoltn1.pdf
The Declaration of Independence	declare.doc	declare.pdf
The American Revolution	revoltn2.doc	revoltn2.pdf
Early Congresses	congress.doc	congress.pdf
The Constitution of the United States	constutn.doc	constutn.pdf
The Bill of Rights	billrght.doc	billrght.pdf

JPEG Files

The images found throughout the book are also provided on the Teacher Resource CD. See pages 141–143 for image descriptions, credits, and filenames.

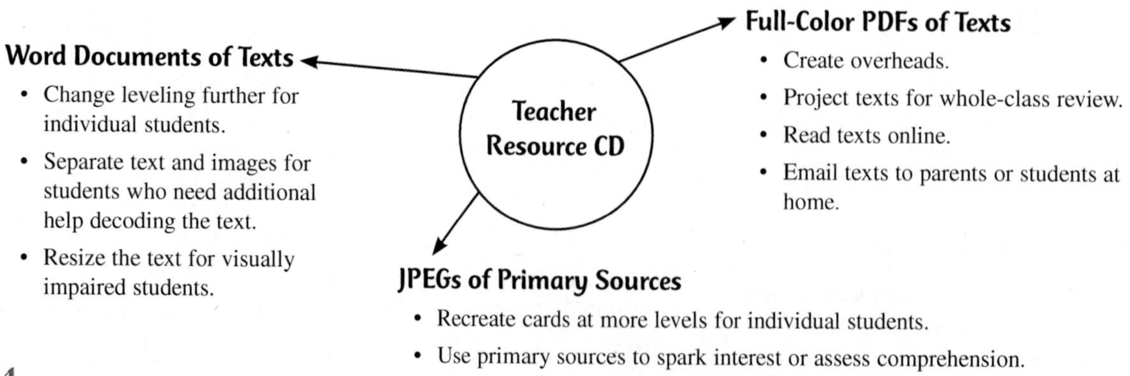

Teacher Resource CD

Word Documents of Texts

- Change leveling further for individual students.
- Separate text and images for students who need additional help decoding the text.
- Resize the text for visually impaired students.

Full-Color PDFs of Texts

- Create overheads.
- Project texts for whole-class review.
- Read texts online.
- Email texts to parents or students at home.

JPEGs of Primary Sources

- Recreate cards at more levels for individual students.
- Use primary sources to spark interest or assess comprehension.